threadless

threadless

ten years of t-shirts from
the world's most inspiring
online design community

Jake Nickell

Abrams Image
New York

Shondi. This book is for you.
The only person who has shared
this wild ride with me since day
one. I'm so happy our children
will feel this same love.

To all of you who participate—artists, staffers,
bloggers, scorers—without you, Threadless would
be nothing.

Cataloging-in-Publication Data has been applied for and may be
obtained from the Library of Congress.

ISBN 978-0-8109-9610-6

Text and images copyright © 2010, **skinnyCorp**

Created and produced by **Harris + Wilson**
Designed by **A-Side Studio**

Typeset in **AauxPro** and **Archer**
Printed and bound in China by **Imago**
10 9 8 7 6 5 4 3 2 1

Abrams Image books are available at special discounts when
purchased in quantity for premiums and promotions as well
as fundraising or educational use. Special editions can also be
created to specification. For details, contact specialmarkets@
abramsbooks.com, or the address below.

THE ART OF BOOKS SINCE 1949
115 West 18th Street
New York, NY 10011
www.abramsbooks.com

CONTENTS

2000
–
2004

01

More than anything, designing t-shirts to submit made my middle school self elated! *Downpour* was the product of my earliest obsession with design and graphic art.

Downpour
by **Scott Giblin** aka **Myxxoma**, USA

Score: 2.78/5 by 266 people

02

I've always been inspired by zoology and fantasy—the real world and then what it becomes when you give it a twist of crazy. Also, jackalopes and demon bunnies are never not awesome.

Odd but Cute
by **Jamie Parris** aka **azrielen**, USA

Score: 2.84/5 by 294 people

03

Caesar (from the movie *Planet of the Apes*): "It's the slave's right to punish his persecutor. . . . Tonight, we have seen the birth of the Planet of the Apes!"

Monkey Attack
by **Gabriel Suchowolski** aka **microbians**, Spain

Score: 3.39/5 by 356 people

07

I've always thought that people with a gruff exterior are actually nice people—just misunderstood—and I wanted to find a way to show that. Plus, who doesn't like drawing a disembodied head on a pike now and then?

Shadow Bunny
by **David Huyck** aka **BoM**, USA

Score: 2.74/5 by 250 people

08

Trying to explain this would be entirely futile.

Consumable
by **Olly Moss** aka **Woss**, UK

Score: 3.05/5 by 459 people

09

This tee makes anyone instantly ten times hotter.

Rachel Gottesman aka **Rachel Ray Gun**

Summer Wind
by **Joachim Baan**, Netherlands

Score: 3.19/5 by 308 people

13

Hi! This design is made for hugs!

Mmm . . . Oranges!
by **Julia Kostreva** aka **vwoop**, USA

Score: 2.11/5 by 245 people

14

There is no way I could surpass the quality of this quote by my captain, Don Van Vliet: "I think that most of the things there are to be learned can be learned from animals."

Permafrost Pollution
by **Viktor Hachmang** aka **Viktor**, Netherlands

Score: 3.47/5 by 388 people

15

It says "Hultsfred 2003" on the tape. Hultsfred was at the time Sweden's largest music festival. The design is basically a music and festival celebration. The tee is inspired by the 1980s and nostalgia for the cassette tape.

Blandband Deluxe
by **Joakim Jansson** aka **1-UP**, Norway

Score: 2.88/5 by 323 people

It's not about eating at all! It's all about stirring, maybe even causing a commotion. People are loading trash into their brains watching TV, living a consumer-zombie life, and maybe we can do something about that, wake them up.

Stir It Up

by **345**, Netherlands

Score: 2.81/5 by 488 people

Clearly, Threadless started the cassette nostalgia movement.

Kristen Studard
aka **hello_kristen**

God Was a Gardener

by **Nathan Flood** aka **Ngin**, USA

Score: n/a

Ooh, plague chic!
Sick is the new sexy!

Kristen Studard
aka **hello_kristen**

Outbreak Girl

by **Joanne Lim** aka **girl_friday**, Singapore

Score: 2.55/5 by 431 people

The placement is what really makes this design special. Great negative space that one might assume is all black smoke. Tuck it in and you have a burning man in your pants.

Bob Nanna aka **BNannas**

Burn

by **Cicero**, USA

Score: 2.74/5 by 445 people

In the fall from the air
The long slide from grace and
With grace
In the midsummer sky blue
of everywhere
To drift on the dream.

Lee Klein

Puppet Ballet

by **Henri-Pierre Trocherie** aka **star69**, France

Score: 2.72/5 by 163 people

When I first created my little blue zombie guy I had no idea how popular he would become. For me he was simply a small spot of indulgence for my love of schlocky horror, but somehow those big, dead, lifeless eyes seem to speak to people.

Corporate Zombie

by **Nik Holmes** aka **NikHolmes**, UK

Score: 2.55/5 by 332 people

I originally drew *She Doesn't Even Realize* for my drawing site, stupidpictures.net, back in 2002. I decided to submit the design to Threadless on a whim and am still amazed at the response it got. . . . I still occasionally get emails from people who enjoy the design and it totally makes my day every time!

She Doesn't Even Realize

by **Dave Fass** aka **lonesquid**, USA

Score: 3.06/5 by 453 people

I sketched that little psycho all the time. A friend of mine saw it and said: "Man, submit this to Threadless." I was like, "Thread-what?" I gave it a try and the end of the story is that the success encouraged me to keep illustrating and start a career as a successful designer and illustrator.

Sad Psycho

by **Michael Fuchs** aka **mr.fox**, Germany

Score: 2.75/5 by 477 people

I wanted the look to be very straightforward and just serve as a vehicle for a surreal concept. I knew that it would take a second for the idea to register, but when it did, people would (hopefully) get a chuckle out of it. Also, I like ice cream.

Road Block

by **Justen Renyer** aka **El Skel**, USA

Score: 2.84/5 by 361 people

THE ACCIDENTAL BUSINESS

Threadless was never intended to be a business. When Jacob DeHart and I started out it was all just a hobby —a fun thing to do for the other designers we were friends with.

The online design scene I was a part of in 2000 was a tiny, tight-knit group experimenting with computers, code, and art. Everyone seemed to know each other. We'd post projects and challenges on forums; we'd bounce ideas off each other, work together, and put up the results. There wasn't a ton of straight-up socializing: everything seemed to be attached to some sort of creative project.

The seed of Threadless came from a t-shirt design competition on dreamless.org for an event in London called the New Media Underground Festival. I entered, and won—though I never did get one of those tees with my design on it.

In an instant messaging conversation I said to Jacob that it would be fun to have an ongoing competition where people could always submit t-shirt designs, and we would print the best ones. And that was the start. We posted our first call for entries as a thread on the Dreamless forum that night: from idea to implementation in just a few hours.

After picking our first winners, we each put in $500. Around $200 was spent on a lawyer to set up a company, and we invested the rest in printing the first batch of tees. We built a real website to sell them on and this was when we introduced the voting system. Typically, a score of 3.0 and above was a great score, and still is today. But it's not just high scores that get printed. Sometimes we look for controversial designs that get a ton of zeros and a ton of fives (but have a mediocre average score), or designs that ensure we have plenty of variety on the site.

For the first two years of Threadless, every penny from selling tees went into printing more tee designs. We didn't even take a salary or cut of sales.

At that time I was going to art school part-time, and working a full-time job as a web developer. Jacob and my girlfriend, Shondi (now my wife), both went to school full-time at Purdue University, which was about two-and-a-half hours away from my base in Chicago. Shondi would come up every weekend and help to ship orders. Sometimes Jacob would come too. Later on I convinced him to quit school; I got him a job at the place where I worked as a web developer, and we began ▸

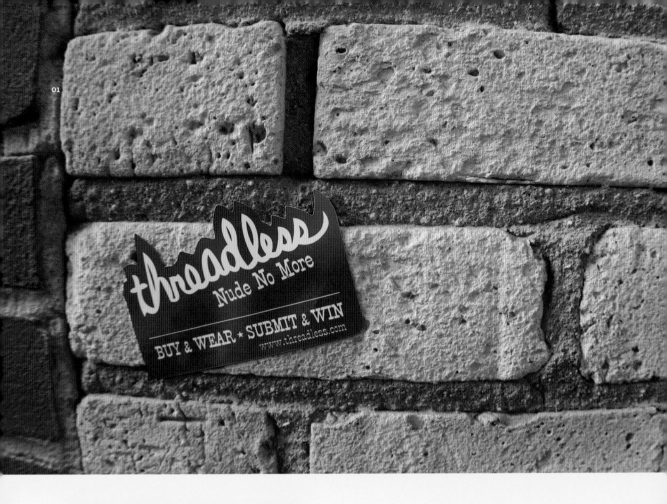

01

FOR THE FIRST TWO YEARS, EVERY PENNY FROM SELLING TEES WENT INTO PRINTING MORE TEE DESIGNS

02

01 Very early on we included free Threadless stickers in every order.

02 The place (*sans* desk) where Threadless started—the corner of my 400-square-foot apartment. Shot with the crappiest camera phone available back then.

root
dreamless.org ├ 03 - dreamless riots
│ ├ London - New Media Underground Festival - November 25th - 27th

shipping orders on our lunch break. It was around this time that people began referring to us as "the Jakes."

I had been building websites professionally since 1996, when, aged sixteen, I worked at the local Internet service provider in my hometown of Crown Point, Indiana. By 2002 I had quit my day job, dropped out of art school, and started my own web agency called skinnyCorp, with Threadless continuing to build under the skinnyCorp umbrella. We moved Threadless out of my apartment and into a 900-square-foot office.

The printing schedule for the tees was very erratic. It was completely based on how much money was in the bank. As soon as we sold out of the last batch of tees, new designs were printed. In 2000, we would print new tees every couple of months. By 2004, we were printing new tees every week. These were truly limited editions, and if they didn't sell, it would be a long time until we could print more.

But in 2003, we had our first real taste of success—a significant amount of revenue. By 2004, Threadless was large enough for us to fire all of our outside clients, focus on our own projects one hundred

percent, and move into a larger warehouse space. Jacob and I also began teaching a course at the Art Institute of Chicago. That made us feel a little better about dropping out of school.

During the early years of Threadless, the t-shirt designs mostly appealed to the design crowd—they weren't mainstream. The most amazing thing about this book is seeing the tees change over time; seeing the growth of Threadless not just through revenue or community size, but in the style shifts and design trends.

It's hard to express how important the design community is to Threadless. It was the reason Jacob and I started, but we were doing a ton of other things for the community as well. When Dreamless "burned the village" (shut down), we started a new forum called yayhooray.com, which we continue to run today. We put on monthly events in Chicago called Anonymous Federated that attracted a few hundred people: flying in a designer to tell their story and show their work. We invited big-name artists to design tees for Threadless, and to become members of the community themselves.

WE'VE ALWAYS HAD AN INCREDIBLY INTERNATIONAL AUDIENCE, RIGHT FROM THE BEGINNING

There has always been an incredibly international audience, right from the beginning. London was the number one city we shipped to for the first few years, more than any US city. This was really cool for us, a company based in the middle of the country, and run by two dudes from small towns.

We also shared our office space with other designers and developers, including Charles Forman (founder of omgpop.com), Nando Costa (nandocosta.com), and Jeffrey Kalmikoff. Jeffrey actually went on to become a huge part of Threadless. He started out doing a lot of design work on our earlier client projects. By 2004 we combined forces, and Jacob, Jeffrey, and I basically ran the business as a team.

As web developers, we spent a lot of time working on our website. We would completely redesign it every few months, just for fun. It was cool, playing around with different interfaces, and we did a lot of innovative things in this way. The core model of Threadless remained the same, and still does today, but the website has undergone a lot of changes.

By the end of 2004, we fully realized that Threadless had huge potential to become a significant business. We started to focus more on it. We took a step back, and looked at what we were doing right, and how we were able to build such an incredible business almost accidentally.

01 **The design that inspired Threadless was an event t-shirt for the New Media Underground Festival in London.**

02 **Here come "the Jakes"—Jacob and me hitting the streets of NYC soon after starting Threadless.**

03 **Our first office dog, Norman, looking cute in the t-shirt shelves.**

04 **Chuck Anderson, now a big-name designer, made this sweet banner for us!**

THE FIRST TEE

I first met Jemma and Dustin (pictured opposite) back on Dreamless in 2000. Jemma has since posted thousands of design explorations on her aesthetic playground, prate.com. We were very lucky to have her submit her *Prate* design, which became the first-ever Threadless tee printed. A few years later, Dustin and Jemma hooked up and got married. Dustin also designed a few Threadless tees and even worked for Threadless curating our Select line. The original *Upso* tee is one of my personal favorites. As Dustin says: "It expresses the idea that we all are going to die, so we might as well enjoy ourselves as much as we can while we are alive." **Jake Nickell**

Jemma There once was a super-secret message board (dreamless.org) for web designers, programmers, and "net-artists," where many friendships, collabs, and projects were born. While most of the discussions happened online, there was also a good deal of face-to-face time. We would get together for drinks in the cities we lived in and at conferences in London, Rotterdam . . . all over. I met "the Jakes" at a small conference in Chicago, and some time later they asked me to submit a Prate tee for their launch competition, which I kindly did.
Dustin From day one I was pretty obsessed with the concept of Threadless. I knew of the dudes that started it from the Dreamless message board. I was really surprised and excited when Threadless asked me to make a t-shirt design [*Upso*] that bypassed the regular submission process. While my work has changed and progressed a lot over the years, I still get excited when I see someone wearing my old design.

Upso (left)

by **Dustin Hostetler** aka **upso**, USA

Prate (right)

by **Jemma Hostetler (née Gura)** aka **lentil**, USA

THE FIRST SUBMISSIONS

These five designs were submitted, along with *Prate* (see pages 16–17), to the first-ever Threadless competition—which actually took place within a thread on the online art forum, Dreamless, and before we had scoring. Threadless.com didn't even exist yet! **Jake Nickell**

Evil Mother Fucking Web Design

by **Livenootrac**, USA

Neonmedia 1

by **Eric Kelly** aka **Count**, USA

Dead Sexy Designer

by **Scott McCready** aka **smccready**, USA

Pixel-Banjomonstar

by **Jay Zehngebot** aka **moltar**, USA

Destroy Nifkin

by **Michael Raichelson** aka **Nifkin**, USA

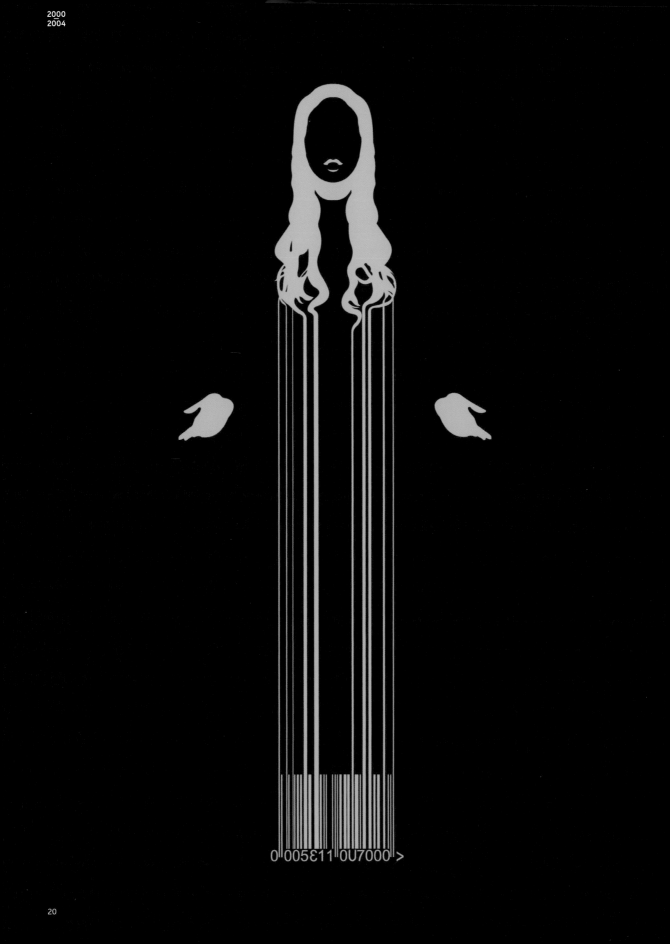

5311 0U7 (opposite)

by **Christopher Moorby** aka **Multiple Moorby**, UK

Score: 2.92/5 by 400 people

I Like Lions Too (above)

by **Gregory Durrell** aka **Xrtions**, Canada

Score: 2.91/5 by 576 people

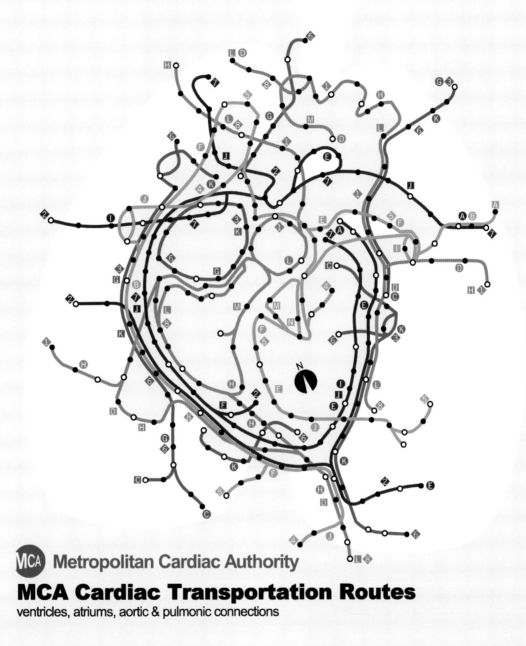

![MCA] **Metropolitan Cardiac Authority**

MCA Cardiac Transportation Routes
ventricles, atriums, aortic & pulmonic connections

Radios (opposite)	**Follow It** (above)
by **Dan Terry** aka **megadan**, USA	by **Philip Gray** aka **__pg**, USA
Score: 2.67/5 by 302 people	Score: 2.48/5 by 215 people

Flowers in the Attic (opposite)
by **Jason Byron Nelson** aka **jbyron**, USA
Score: 3.79/5 by 293 people

Afternoon Delight (above)
by **Chris Bishop** aka **chrisbishop**, USA
Score: 2.47/5 by 272 people

they lied to us

this was supposed to be the future

where is my jetpack,

where is my robotic companion,
where is my dinner in pill form,
where is my hydrogen fueled automobile,
where is my nuclear-powered levitating house,

where is my cure for this disease

FROM THREADLESSLAND TO OBAMATOWN

John Slabyk's first design, *Damn Scientists*, is a timeless Threadless tee. It still gets reprinted today. Next, he designed a Type Tee based on the slogan "Girls should have the right to vote." Fast forward a few years and he's working as the art director on Barack Obama's presidential campaign! Considering that this is arguably the best designed campaign in history, that's one incredible achievement. It was also cool to find out that the eagle featured in John's Type Tee is now a design element on the official White House website. You can catch it at whitehouse.gov. **Jake Nickell**

Damn Scientists (opposite)

by **John Slabyk** aka **S2o**, USA

Score: 2.77/5 by 436 people

THIS IS NO ABOUT T-SHIRTS

HEY, IT'S NOT EVEN ABOUT CROWDSOURCING, OR NEW BUSINESS MODELS, OR THE INTERNET.

Seth Godin

It's about being willing to fail and relishing the idea of being different.

Ever since I encountered Threadless, and then particularly after I had lunch with "the Jakes," I've been in awe of their willingness to be wrong and their desire to be different.

Different = risky. Risky today = safe.

The magic of what Threadless has built lies in its apparent recklessness. But it's not reckless, of course. General Motors was reckless, wasting billions on boring cars they knew wouldn't sell. Circuit City was reckless, rolling out giant temples of average, knowing that people could find stuff just as average right down the street.

If you page through this book, you'll see example after example of love, and art, and joy . . . but not a lot of fear. Fearlessness and recklessness might appear to be related, but they're not. Jake is fearless. He understands that the actual risks are fairly small, and given that the risks are accounted for, he dives in. Reckless business people, on the other hand, are dangerous because they risk everything all out of proportion to the upside.

So, my hat's off to the crazy (smart) people at Threadless. Here's a company that hires the unhirable, codes the uncodable, markets the unmarketable. It did so during a time when everyone else was wringing their hands and whining, and they did it with flair and aplomb.

Can I have my free t-shirt now?

Seth Godin is the author of twelve international bestsellers including *Purple Cow*, *Tribes*, and *Linchpin*. His books have been translated into more than thirty languages and have helped transform the way we think about work, marketing, and change. Seth writes the world's most popular and influential marketing blog. He is also the founder of squidoo.com.

I had been put on hold by a call center when this Post-it note doodle in black Biro popped into my head. I was living in England—squirrels were a big novelty as we don't get them in New Zealand. I think the ultimate compliment is seeing how much it has been ripped off. It was especially surreal when I found fakes being sold in a Bangkok market!

Nuts!

by **Barnaby Bocock** aka **hey_barn**, New Zealand

Score: 3.07/5 by 533 people

STRICLTY_PROHIBITED

07
KILL ZONE

HE_Shoot_DE

ABNORMALBEHAVIORCHILD

CAREERS BEYOND THREADLESS

One of the most exciting things about Threadless is following the other work of the artists involved. Almost every day some amazing project or product comes across my desk that involves a Threadless artist. It has been fantastic watching people's careers take off (see pages 26–27). Two of my favorite examples are Tokidoki and Niko Stumpo. Early on we asked them to design tees for Threadless outside the usual submission process; they then went on to start their own amazing product lines. You can check them out at tokidoki.it and weareaiko.com **Jake Nickell**

Tokidoki (opposite)   **He_Shoot** (above)
by **Simone Legno** aka **Tokidoki**, Italy   by **Niko Stumpo** aka **abnormal**, Italy

MP(3) (opposite)

by **Matthew Fleming** aka **flembo**, USA

Score: 3.24/5 by 272 people

Bleeding Heart (above)

by **Craig Brickles** aka **Brickboy80**, UK

Score: 2.39/5 by 399 people

Location: Chicago, IL, USA

Member since July 2003

I had a well-documented childhood. My parents are photographers, and we had a darkroom in our house in Baton Rouge, Louisiana. They are amazing parents. I'm their only child, so they dragged me to all the art openings they could. I resisted every time, but as much as I fought it, some of this art and culture must have stuck—thanks, Mom and Dad.

At school I had a bump on the top of my middle finger from drawing so much. I filled dozens of sketchbooks with pencil drawings of cars, basketball shoes, animals, and superheroes.

My college was definitely known more for its football than its art. But I did have some inspiring professors who helped me get a hold of the basics: kerning, Letraset, Swiss design, Garamond, negative space, acetate, Adobe, Saul Bass. I did my best to soak it all up like a sponge.

In a way, my professors also helped me discover Threadless. I read a blurb about it in *Communication Arts* magazine, wasting time in a Barnes & Noble book store while I was supposed to be researching some web project. That night I made my first t-shirt design. It was horrible, but of course in my mind it was an amazing, original idea. There would be a heart (really shoddily vectored in Macromedia Freehand) printed on the sleeve—thus it would be a heart on your sleeve.

People destroyed that first design in the comments, which was awesome. It got me hooked. So then I wanted to prove to all these cleverly named faceless wince-inducing commenters that I could do something they liked. In the next two months I submitted eight more designs. ▸

ROSS ZIETZ *aka* **ARZIE13**

01

My scores were steadily climbing and the comments were becoming less and less hurtful. Then came my ninth sub, *Squeaked*: a running elephant on the front and a group of mice in pursuit on the back. It was not the prettiest design, but it was a clever enough use of the t-shirt medium. That was my first print. If I could rework any of my designs, that would be the one. I was still learning vectors back then—that file is pretty nasty.

At this point I was spending more time on Threadless subs than on my school projects, which turned out not to be such a bad idea. After graduating I procrastinated and traveled a bit then applied to a couple of ad agencies in New Orleans. I was about to accept an offer when Jake posted a blog about Threadless looking to hire a multi-purpose worker. I think this basically meant janitor.

When I flew to see Threadless in Chicago the river was dyed green. It was St. Patrick's Day. I was "interviewed" at an Irish bar downtown where I met the whole crew—all eight of them. I was a bit Internet star struck. Everyone was nice—they laughed when I said "y'all," and I was offered a job the next day. That was six years ago.

The surprising thing about the Threadless office is that although it resembles Pee-Wee's Playhouse, we still get a lot of stuff done. I'm now the art director, and looking forward to going to work each morning. I still sub designs—that was a stipulation of accepting.

My last name means jack rabbit in some old Czech dialect, and I have always been a bit obsessed with them. So I got a home screen-printing kit and decided to make a simple one-color logo I could screen on to some shirts.

01 **Woody** (personal work)
02 **Bigfoot Riding Nessie** (personal work)
03 **rainBOW** (Manifest Equality Art Show)
04 **Lampdog** (personal work)

You can see some of Ross's Threadless designs on pages 45 (**12, 16**), 54, 72 (**01**), 128 (**15**), and 206.

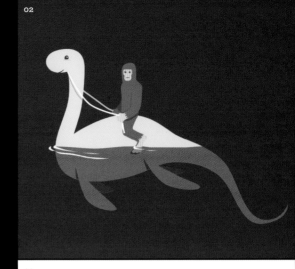

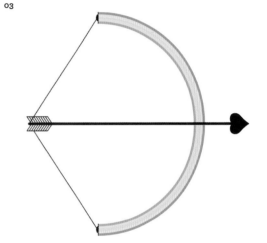

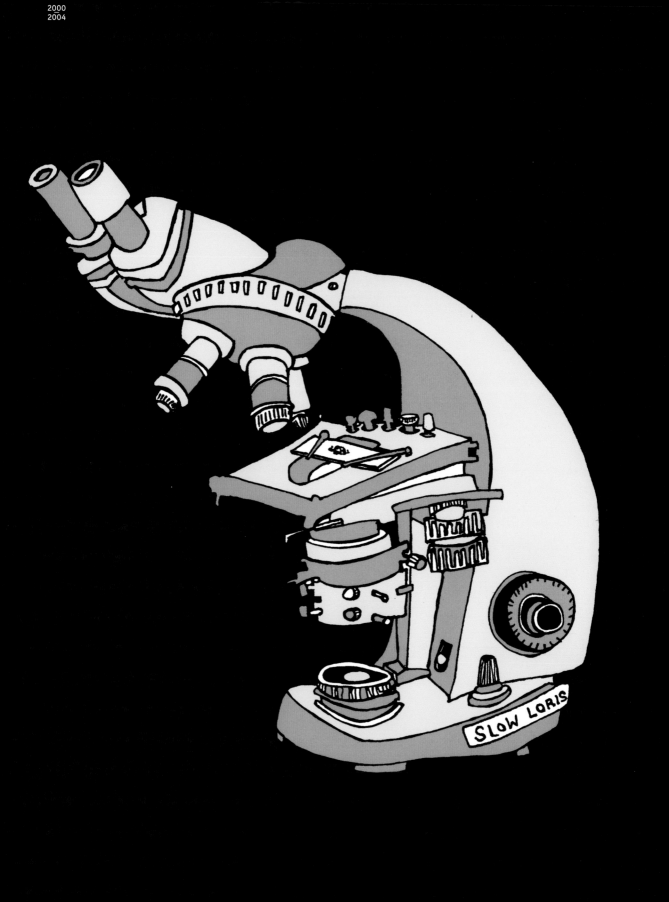

pg. 432, Scientific Tools (opposite)
by **Jessica Lynch** aka **slow loris shirts**, USA
Score: 2.32/5 by 485 people

Doodle (above)
by **Stephen Carr** aka **monkeynotes**, UK
Score: 2.69/5 by 117 people

01

One of those ideas that just comes out of the blue, it was originally about the ark sinking and animals in lifeboats. The iceberg was a last-minute addition but added so much more to the story.

Biblical Disaster
by **Glenn Jones** aka **Glennz**, New Zealand

Score: 3.94/5 by 1,239 people

02

I got a pony for Christmas one year and I worked at the jelly bean factory. Everyone was jealous of my pony. Then one day, my pony disappeared. It was never to be found again

David aka **this_boy**

My Little Pony
by **Kenneth Lavallee** aka **kennnnnnnnnn**, Canada

Score: 2.03/5 by 1,239 people

03

Gingerbread men are a good subject for humor. This started out as a cookie cutter concept, but it evolved as I drew it. I think It would be any gingerbread man's nightmare to only get half cut out.

Gingerbread Nightmares
by **Glenn Jones** aka **Glennz**, New Zealand

Score: 3.68/5 by 626 people

07

I did the two illustrations separately and then put them together accidentally and loved it. Later I came up with the title, after drinking some delicious Robitussin.

Captain Bellyflop Strikes Again
by **Alan Ivester Spach** aka **catdogpigduck**, USA

Score: 3.23/5 by 1,137 people

08

Naughty night-napping ninjas fight for future freedom!

Pillow Fight
by **Fiona Lee** aka **fOi**, Australia

Score: 3.71/5 by 617 people

09

Southbound Pachyderm is inspired by a Primus song of the same title. The lyrics refer to them taking to the sky. I thought the title had a nice ring to it and was interested in exploring the flying elephant motif visually. The tattoo reads: NUTZ.

Southbound Pachyderm
by **Frank Barbara** aka **franx**, Canada

Score: 3.21/5 by 574 people

13

Seriously, who can't be inspired by love?

So Lovely
by **Sven Grothe** aka **sveninho**, Belgium

Score: 2.47/5 by 418 people

14

Vinyl, files, and cassettes. Mr. Wheeler, you nailed it!

Bob Nanna aka **BNannas**

Music Box
by **Phil Wheeler** aka **conan doyle**, Spain

Score: 2.22/5 by 982 people

15

The first title for the design was *Moby vs. Ikea*. I wanted to show something old and iconic confronting something new and temporary, and then eventually coexisting together. I changed the title to be less specific and more fun.

Moby Was a Consumer
by **Jim Slatton** aka **jimbrowski**, USA

Score: 3.38/5 by 604 people

04

Stabby McKnife started life as an illustration in one of Kevin Cornell's many sketchbooks. He was created as a narrative on how fast-food companies market to kids. Kevin gave me permission to use Stabby and he has been in our hearts ever since . . . not literally I hope, but you get the idea.

Stabby McKnife
by **Springfish**, USA

Score: 2.89/5 by 886 people

I had to illustrate the slogan "Vikings are just Swedish pirates" for the now defunct OMG tees. I guess I had Ikea on the brain. . . .

Vikings Are Just Swedish Pirates
by **Olly Moss** aka **Woss**, UK

Score: n/a

This still remains one of my favorite designs. I thought it would be easier for him to use a pay phone to call home rather than have the hassle of creating a new communication device.

Calling Home
by **Glenn Jones** aka **Glennz**, New Zealand

Score: 3.63/5 by 516 people

This shirt has a zombie and it's green. Green because that is the color of most zombies. This is the perfect shirt for St. Patrick's Day because it is so green.

Of the Dead
by **Justin White** aka **jublin**, USA

Score: 2.83/5 by 1,041 people

Pumpkin pies, sunshine, golden times, time fades, but love will always remain.

Time Fades
by **Samuel Lara Hernández** aka **label**, Mexico

Score: 3.66/5 by 1,098 people

I love the idea of Nessie, but I love the idea of a sneaky squid even more.

Loch Ness Imposter
by **Ross Zietz** aka **arzie13**, USA

Score: 3.77/5 by 1,535 people

A simple ode to a T-bone. Oddly enough, vegetarians like this shirt just as much as the meat eaters.

Piece of Meat
by **Ross Zietz** aka **arzie13**, USA

Score: 2.42/5 by 428 people

To be honest I just looked at the toaster and my mind did the rest—it has a persistent problem with making every single inanimate object appear cute.

We're Toast
by **Natalie Hurtenbach** aka **tunastar**, USA

Score: 3.30/5 by 591 people

I made that design in high school because I really wanted to win.

Vampire Orthodontics
by **Ilia Ovechkin** aka **olympic**, USA

Score: 1.95/5 by 204 people

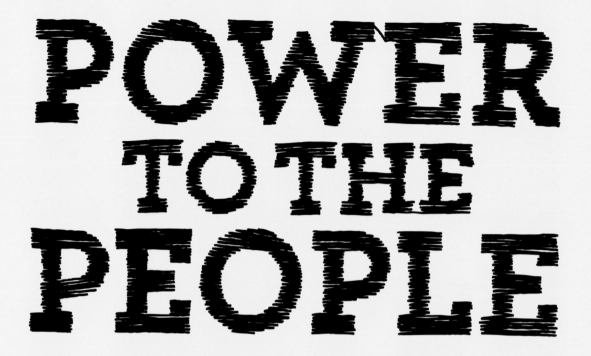

POWER TO THE PEOPLE

This was the year that Threadless became very "real" for us. Having taken the plunge of firing all our clients, we now depended on Threadless for our own personal income. We also had employees dedicated to the project. It was time to start thinking of this as a business rather than a hobby.

The moment that became crystal clear was when we were invited to speak at a user innovation conference at the Massachusetts Institute of Technology (MIT). We really didn't know what we were getting ourselves into. Apparently, some people at the school had been researching this new idea of "user innovation," and "crowdsourcing," and came across us: the first business they'd really seen implement it in the real world. Huge businesses such as General Mills and Pitney Bowes were represented at the conference, discussing this new business model. We were the only ones who actually ran our business that way.

And we thought we were just making cool designs with friends online.

Learning more about what we were doing from people with business degrees at MIT gave us a nice

extra chunk of confidence. We got to work. We started hiring a lot of talented people outside our friend circle. Brianne started in customer service and now heads up the department. Ross applied as our janitor and went on to become our art director. We hired Harper and Ivan for technology, with Harper eventually becoming our CTO. Bob and Lance started in the warehouse, which Lance now runs, and Bob is currently head of promotions. Shondi, my wife, did most of the hiring, and focused on getting our operations up to par, particularly our accounting, customer service, and warehouse.

All of a sudden we had to do boring, lame things like payroll and book-keeping. We substantially increased the prize money awarded to artists, introduced a tee of the month club, and launched our "Loves" design challenges (see pages 140–141). We began doing sponsored challenges with magazines, bands, and groups we liked, began a podcast, and even put up a billboard in New York City, on one of the busiest corners in the world (see pages 54–55).

We also started new businesses outside Threadless. Like nakedandangry.com, a site where ▸

ALL OF A SUDDEN WE HAD TO DO BORING, LAME THINGS LIKE PAYROLL AND BOOK-KEEPING

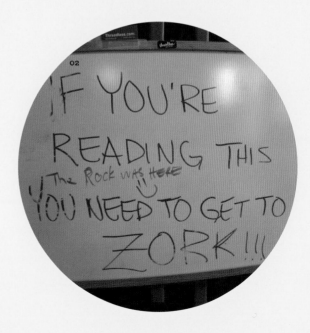

01 This was our first real "atrium," which all our offices now have. The MAME arcade cabinet on the right has more than 5,000 games!

02 The culture of random nonsense EVERYWHERE is well in evidence.

01

WE WERE PRINTING SIX NEW DESIGNS PER WEEK, AND EVERYTHING WE MADE SOLD

artists submit design patterns that are then made into products such as ties, wallpaper, handbags, wallets, umbrellas, and dish sets. With Naked and Angry we learned that when the product range is so broad, it is better to collaborate with companies that are already successful within each product category.

We started OMG Clothing, which later turned into the successful slogan-based typetees.com. Then there was iparklikeanidiot.com, a hilarious goofy side project. We sell bumper stickers that say, "I Park Like an Idiot" in packs from twenty to a hundred. This was born from our collective frustration toward bad parkers who take up multiple spots—which is especially annoying when you live in a big city.

The year was huge for Threadless. We grew so much. In 2004 our total revenue was around $1.5 million,

and in 2005 it jumped to $6.5 million. We really discovered the potential of Threadless during this year. There were a lot of stumbling blocks that came with the success. Lots of shipping delays due to growing pains in our warehouse, and a fair amount of drama in the workplace.

Even with this growth, our supply still never really caught up with the demand in 2005. We were printing six new designs per week, and everything we made sold. Everything. If we printed a design and put it up for sale, that meant it would sell out within six months.

It makes sense. It's simple. If we only make the stuff people tell us they'd like to buy before we even make it, then we should be able to sell it once we do make it.

As Threadless "grew up," there was one incredibly important element that was clear with everyone, and still is today. Threadless is a community of people first,

a t-shirt store second. Most day-to-day visitors on Threadless are not there to shop. They are there to submit designs, score designs, talk in the forums, read interviews, browse the photo galleries, and just generally be inspired by other members in the community.

There may be these new, fancy words and ideas to describe what we're doing in an academic way, but we try not to let it change us. Threadless really is just a giant group of friends making cool designs; not an "innovative crowdsourcing platform."

We found it a little awkward trying to stay as ourselves, when we were being defined by influential magazines and business schools. But I think we found our groove, and I think we've kept self-aware, despite all the chatter.

01 Pete and Jeff get into a heated debate over a customer service issue. This is our third office space.

02 A batch of tees ready to be shipped out around the world.

03 On a trip to LA with Jeffrey, I bought a cheap fur coat and a bag of oranges, which I spilled all over the hotel lobby!

E=MC Escher (opposite)

by **Tom Burns** aka **tomburns**, USA

Score: 2.95/5 by 1,080 people

Mona Prankster (above)

by **Herman Lee** aka **dhectwenty**, Hong Kong

Score: 1.75/5 by 431 people

PANDAS FOR PEACE

My first idea was to have a King Kong–type giant panda climbing the side of a building while swatting at planes, but pandas seem so peaceful to me. They just want to eat, sleep, and make baby pandas. So I went with a more peaceful approach and tried to make it seem like the panda doesn't know it's causing any trouble. Lots of people seemed to think this was an anti-war shirt, which is also fine by me. I love when people can pull many different meanings from a single design. I'm happy to say the giant panda actually got to fulfill his King Kong–style destiny and was on the side of a building as a Threadless billboard in NYC. **Ross Zietz**

Pandamonium

by **Ross Zietz** aka **arzie13,** USA

Score: 3.53/5 by 458 people

Sitting out a couple summers back
while drawing in my sketchbook,
I gazed over at my wheelbarrow and
had the strangest vision: She was there.
Soaking up the sun in a wheelbarrow
bubble tub! And that was that.

Barrow Bath

by **Josh Tuininga** aka **tuniguts**, USA

Score: 3.11/5 by 1,117 people

Location: Auckland, New Zealand

Member since July 2004

It's always blown me away that I can be down here in New Zealand and have an audience all over the world. I started designing for Threadless at a good time, just before the Threadless "Big Bang." So when it exploded into the mainstream I was able to ride that wave too. The exposure was incredible.

It wouldn't be exaggerating to say that Threadless changed my life. I'd happily climbed the ladder in a design career for fifteen years, then as soon as I got to where I thought I wanted to be, I left it all to draw t-shirts. I take great pride in what I have achieved on Threadless, and would like to think that my illustration style and some of my designs helped forge a bit of Threadless's identity too.

When I signed up I couldn't think of anything better than Glennz as my username—Glenn from NZ. Amazingly creative! When I decided to open my own tee-shirt store I couldn't come up with anything else either, so I just added "Tees" to the end of it. Glennz Tees is based in Austin, Texas, which is the location of my friends and business partners who make Glennz Tees happen.

My work has definitely had a bit of a love-hate relationship with Threadless voters. My style didn't really change too much: some liked it, and some saw that as a negative. I think that consistency helped build an identity for me, so people knew my work just by seeing it. Unfortunately for some others it created the "that looks like a glennz" comments. Hopefully my work makes a few people laugh. ▶

GLENN JONES *aka* GLENNZ

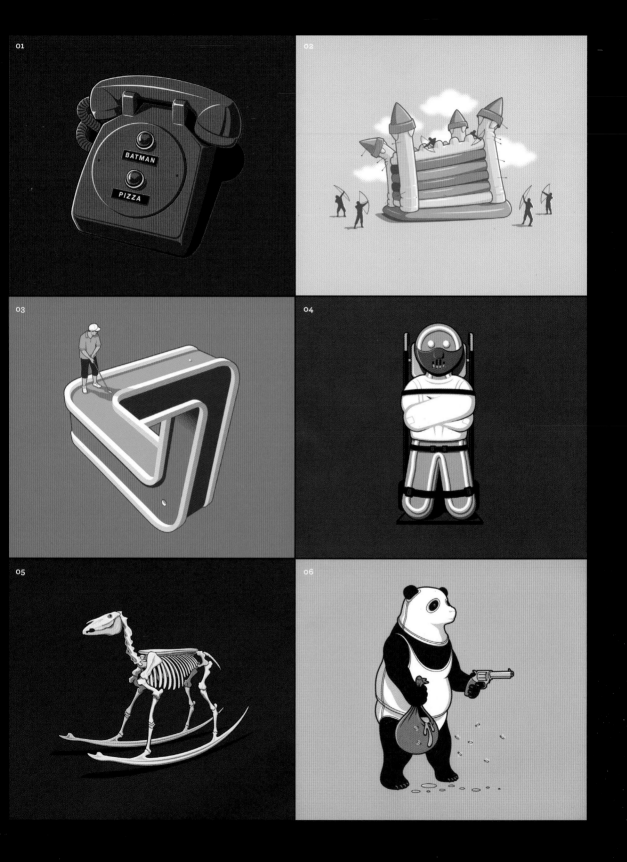

The best ideas come when I'm zoned out, like if I'm driving or running, but I probably only remember about one in five. I do most of my work on the couch, feet up, TV on. My inspiration comes from anywhere and everywhere. The Discovery Channel, and pop culture, always seem to be favorites of mine.

I love vector art—the crisp and smooth lines that can be achieved in Illustrator. I got my start drawing for a newspaper. Working in editorial graphics taught me to convey the theme of an illustration in a clear, understandable way as simply as possible. Less is more.

It's hard to choose my favorites on Threadless. I always liked *MP(3)*, and *Wingtips*, also *Take a Hike*, *Loch Ness Imposter*, and *Bob Shopping*.

The best thing about art is anyone can do it and everyone has their own taste. The possibilities and potential are endless. It can bring all sorts of different people together on the same level, much like Threadless.

I learn stuff every day having my own online store, but I think the main things I would pass on are: *(a)* You'll never be able to make everyone happy, but listen to what people say and try to keep improving. *(b)* Don't try to do it all by yourself. Surround yourself with people who are good at the things you aren't good at. *(c)* Lastly, be patient (I'm not very good at being patient). Some stuff takes time but you get there in the end, so it's worth the wait.

I've always got a kick out of seeing someone wearing one of my tees. When I first started subbing to Threadless the prize money was about $150 so it was never about the money. The idea of people wearing my shirt design all over the world is so cool. I walked past someone wearing one of my tees last week, and I still feel the same way.

01 **Direct Line**
02 **Deflating Defenses**
03 **Puzzled Putter**
04 **Cannibal**
05 **Equus Rockus**
06 **In Disguise**
07 **Organized Food Fight**
(All designs Glennz Tees)

You can see some of Glenn's Threadless designs on pages 44 (01, 03) and 45 (06).

God Hates Techno (opposite)

by **G. Dan Covert** aka **us**, USA

Score: 1.79/5 by 547 people

Ah Munna Eat Choo (above)

by **Nathaniel Kusinitz** aka **BrainMeats**, USA

Score: 2.98/5 by 496 people

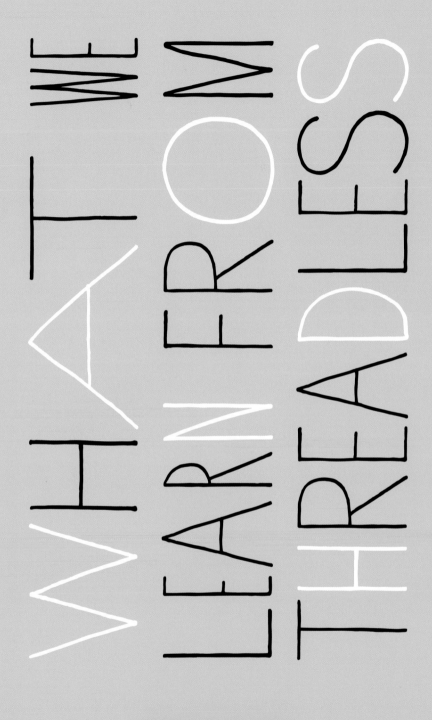

WHAT WE LEARN FROM THREADLESS

Scott Belsky

WHAT IS THREADLESS? IS IT A COMMUNITY? A RETAIL STORE? A REVOLUTIONARY PLAY ON E-COMMERCE? THE ULTIMATE DESIGNER'S PLAYGROUND?

I don't think that Jake and Jacob created Threadless with any one of these definitions in mind. As for the early Threadless users, they did not join the site to make history (or money). Instead, they were in it for the love of the game, just like the founders. They all just wanted to participate.

I have always admired a common ethos among Threadless participants. They value participation as an experience in itself. Exploring the creations of your peers around the world, uploading your own designs, and supporting ingenuity whenever you buy a t-shirt—these are all actions that make Threadless vibrant and engaging. Collectively, these actions have sustained Threadless for a decade. Threadless doesn't drive us. We drive Threadless.

The word "community" is thrown around all too often these days. Every business, school, and interest group proclaims to "own" or "run" a community. The fact is that most of them are missing the point. Threadless doesn't own a community. Threadless participates in a community that is much bigger than Threadless.

We can learn a lot from this understanding. Community is participation. If you offer value and opportunity to a community, you will become a leader within it. Threadless also demonstrates that the best community leaders act as stewards, listening to participants and sometimes making difficult decisions to sustain the ethos.

To me, this is the genius of Threadless.

Scott Belsky is the founder and CEO of Behance and oversees the Behance Network, the leading online platform for creative professionals. He is also the author of *Making Ideas Happen: Overcoming the Obstacles Between Vision and Reality*.

CUTE AND COLORFUL

These designs marked the beginning of a trend—simple, cute, cartoony designs that were also often colorful. They pop really nicely on tees, which is one reason why I think these types of illustrations are still popular today. **Jake Nickell**

Well, This Just Really Sucks . . .

by **Kevin Ryan** aka **kreamy**, USA

Score: 3.26/5 by 1,259 people

Mourning Girl

by **Ben Garraud** aka **bgarraud**, UK

Score: 3.44/5 by 663 people

Ice Cream Mann

by **Romantic Walrus** aka **mrwalrusface**, USA

Score: 2.45/5 by 1,455 people

Cookie Loves Milk

by **Jess Fink** aka **finkenstein**, USA

Score: 3.22/5 by 984 people

You Sank My Battleship

by **Ron Lewis** aka **ronlewis**, USA

Score: 3.66/5 by 232 people

01

Bicycles are fun and gas is expensive.

Infinity MPG

by **Ross Zietz** aka **arzie13**, USA

Score: 2.98/5 by 2,096 people

02

Just tell your kids, "I've been there, done THAT and I've got this t-shirt that you can refer to if you have any further questions."

Birds & the Bees

by **James Pearson, Michael Crawley and Tom Lindsay** aka **studioduplo**, UK

Score: 2.74/5 by 1,963 people

03

Alphabet Zoo is a display of very simple yet identifiable silhouettes of animals in alphabetical order. How we recognize animals isn't complex: anyone of any age can point to the simple shapes and name a creature at hand.

Alphabet Zoo

by **Sara Lee** aka **ibakedesign**, USA

Score: 3.00/5 by 2,415 people

07

"Hi" is just such a banal word, almost meaningless, so I thought it would be fun to treat it ironically and make it exuberant.

HI

by **Ray Fenwick** aka **Ray.**, Canada

Score: 1.76/5 by 2,129 people

08

What better way to express one's animalistic desire to rock than to whip out your rooster for all to admire.

Rock out With Your Cock Out

by **Simon Massey Di Vallazza** aka **francobolli**, Australia

Score: 2.75/5 by 2,143 people

09

The idea is that we all have so many choices in life, like we're standing at a vending machine, but sometimes that thing we really want gets stuck after we put in our money. It's just out of reach, and we're out of change.

Some Choices Are Just out of Reach

by **Rocky Davies** aka **Rockslide**, USA

Score: 2.54/5 by 2,013 people

13

Growing up and having children of my own has exposed me to the relentless bombardment of Saturday morning television advertising. This design is based on the idea of a dark side to the overly cute toys advertised—a side the children didn't see until they grew up.

Ma Lil' Outlaws

by **Clayton Dixon** aka **DEXXON**, New Zealand

Score: 3.32/5 by 1,045 people

14

We're on the Same Level started out as a scribble in the margins of my microeconomics notebook in college. I don't really remember anything I learned in microeconomics, but whenever I see my doodle printed somewhere it makes me glad that class was required.

We're on the Same Level

by **Dud Lawson** aka **dudmatic**, USA

Score: 2.93/5 by 683 people

15

This is one of my favorite Threadless designs. Everyone who sees it loves the juxtaposition between adorable and abominable.

Bob Nanna aka **BNannas**

Bad Teddy

by **Arthur V. Medeiros** aka **plasmanter**, Brazil

Score: 2.92/5 by 2,528 people

04

I was taking an astronomy class at the time and saw a diagram of the electromagnetic spectrum in my textbook. I thought a more artistic representation of it would make an interesting shirt design, and apparently Threadless thought so, too!

Electromagnetic Spectrum
by **Julia Sonmi Heglund** aka **sonmi**, USA

Score: 2.52/5 by 2,408 people

When nature calls, go for a ride! We should enjoy our time, cycling around the park, and keep ourselves surrounded with nature. It's the best time ever!

Nature Call!
by **Yeoh Guan Hong** aka **yeohgh**, China

Score: 2.93/5 by 1,982 people

This was designed during my university days when funneling as much alcohol as possible was pretty awesome. My favorite comment was: "Despicable. I find this in really horrible taste. Can't figure out why so many are finding this funny. It shows a really crass and sexist attitude toward women."

Goldilocks and the Three Beers
by **Matt Hammond** aka **mattnz**, New Zealand

Score: 2.45/5 by 2,181 people

Push bi-poopisanship, or we're all headed for the crapper.

Everyone Poops
by **Chris Lee Jones** aka **tophjones**, USA

Score: 2.46/5 by 2,414 people

This was basically a happy accident, a pattern-drawing exercise that got out of hand when I noticed that it was starting to look a bit like an elephant. It just kinda evolved from there.

Psychedelephant
by **Ole Ivar Rudi** aka **OlliRudi**, Norway

Score: 2.32/5 by 2,039 people

Some cats, like some people, want it all. But, just like people, they sometimes have to face the consequences!

Ambition Killed the Cat
by **Neil Gregory** aka **NGee**, UK

Score: 3.34/5 by 2,276 people

It was just a spur-of-the-moment design that I got lucky with.

You've Got Some Splaining to Do
by **Andy Wilhite** aka **Leroy_Hornblower**, USA

Score: 3.56/5 by 2,607 people

By reversing the scales of two objects you can create something much more interesting and ridiculous, plus bonsai trees are pretty cool as well as being faster and stronger when colored red.

Bonsai Gardener
by **Matt Hammond** aka **mattnz**, New Zealand

Score: 2.88/5 by 1,979 people

Isn't it ironic that a nation sometimes has to wage violent wars in order to bring sovereignty and peace to its people.

Peace and Hate. Can You Tell the Difference?
by **Allan Faustino** aka **alanis**, Philippines

Score: 2.67/5 by 1,970 people

IT'S A REVOLUTION

This was the first year we really needed help in order to continue growing. It wasn't that we needed help to grow, it was that we needed help handling our growth. The holidays in 2005 were embarrassing; so many people didn't get their gifts in time for Christmas. If you placed an order then, it took up to a month for us to even ship it. A major problem. We were also having difficulties with international shipping, with orders getting lost or stuck at customs.

We had a few choices. We could start working with consultants, who would advise us on how to get this kind of stuff done. Or we could outsource the things we weren't that great at, such as order fulfillment. Well, we decided to get someone who knew what they were doing invested in our success by selling a minority stake in the company. This was a way to get the professional help we needed, and it was also nice for Jacob and I to take some money off the table for the portion we sold. (Huge shout out to Jeff over at

Insight Venture Partners, our investor, who has been an amazing source of knowledge when we don't know what to do; not to mention full of awesome ideas we never thought of.)

We were beginning to get a lot of press. We were a really interesting story for business publications, web development blogs, and social media. I still find it crazy that our business model is so revolutionary, when I never finished college, started it as a hobby, and the idea is so incredibly simple. But I guess if I learned to do things the "right" way, Threadless would never have happened.

With the press, we found, came the speaking circuits. Public speaking is not something I enjoy. I've done a ton of it over the years, and I think I'm getting better, but I still get incredibly nervous. I don't do as much of it any more, as I have young children at home; I don't like to be on the road, and I've learned how to say no. But man, in 2006 my whole spring was shot. I couldn't believe so many people wanted to hear about

I GUESS IF I LEARNED TO DO THINGS THE "RIGHT" WAY, THREADLESS WOULD NEVER HAVE HAPPENED

01 One of my favorite product shots for Ilias Karim's tee, *Blog,* inspired by gang symbols. The Threadless gang members: (*clockwise from left*) Jacob, Jeffrey, Harper, and me.

Threadless. Mindblowing! Luckily, Jeffrey, Jacob, and I usually spoke together, or in sets of two. That made it easier. Sometimes these events would be good excuses to travel, too. I even got to visit Copenhagen, to speak at the Danish User-Centered Innovation Lab.

A bunch of cool stuff was happening in our community. One of our printed designers decided he'd start up a forum for other printed designers. They formed a group called the Black Rock Collective, and closed up after they became about forty artists strong. They are still doing collaborations today, and are a force to be reckoned with. A few fan sites started sprouting up as well. One of the best and longest-running is by Chris Cardinal—lovesthreadless.com. Today Chris runs other unofficial Threadless promotions, such as threadcakes.com and threadknits.com.

Around the same time as we sold the minority share to Insight, we moved into a new space. In the first six years of the business, we moved every year. This ▸

01

IT BECAME APPARENT THAT WE WOULD NEED SOME ELECTRIC GO-KARTS TO COVER THE DISTANCES IN THE WAREHOUSE

time we went from about 6,000 square feet to 25,000 square feet. And again, we filled it up fast. It became apparent that we would need some electric go-karts to cover the distances in the warehouse. I was almost killed when I drove one through the snow in our Chicago back alley (there is a pretty hilarious video, as I had a tripod strapped to the front of the kart; look it up). These years were the best for insanity, pranks, and all-around tomfoolery in the workplace.

The one thing we still hadn't really done right yet was to hire new people in the positions that really needed filling. We were stretching ourselves thin. Since we did all of the development on the website and also ran the company, we found ourselves managing during

the day and doing website development at night. It was pure madness. At one point I was pulling all-nighters weekly.

This was the year we introduced two new t-shirt lines. Select is a premium line that we curate, inviting well-known artists we respect to design tees. Type Tees is a submission-based model, only you submit slogans for t-shirts rather than designs.

By the end of 2006, thanks in no small part to my wife, we were operationally solid. Orders were shipped the same day most of the time; always within a couple of days. International shipping got way cheaper and faster. We got better at making the right amount of stuff to sell. Woo-hoo!

01 Some of the guys from the Black Rock Collective: (*from left to right*) Priscilla Wilson, Philip Tseng, Santiago Uceda, Jared Stumpenhorst, Julia Sonmi Heglund, and Justin White.

02 Need more space! The new warehouse tripled the size of the old one.

03 All of our fulfillment operations at this time were very much DIY. A conveyor belt was definitely necessary.

i came to dance

Mosaic Messiah (opposite)
by Peter Peterson aka Pee Pee, New Zealand
Score: 2.57/5 by 2,487 people

I Wanna Dance (above)
by Robert Gould aka Robsoul, USA
Score: 2.18/5 by 2,002 people

HELPING YOU GET THINGS DONE

So, tell us about *Lil' Soap*. **Where did you get the inspiration for him? His style seems like a throwback to an old advertising icon.** Well, I've always done little doodles of creatures that seemed to amuse only me. The idea just popped into my head of inanimate objects being totally into helping you get things done. I came up with my *Cookie Loves Milk* (see page 67) design in a similar fashion. Luckily, Threadless is a place that enjoys my silly ideas as much as I do! **We love that your designs are consistently charming, but not overly cutesy. But what do you think makes** *Lil' Soap* **so successful?** Well . . . everyone can relate, I suppose. At least, everyone who washes their butt! **Have you ever seen** *Lil' Soap* **on a stranger? If so, did you run up to them and shout "I did that!"?** Unfortunately I have never spotted *Lil' Soap* in the wild, unless you count my friends and their babies. I have, however, seen *Cookie Loves Milk* on television *and* tattoos, though, which just blows my mind! **Jess Fink**

Lil' Soap
....
by **Jess Fink** aka **finkenstein**, USA
....
Score: 2.74 by 1,709 people

WHO WILL REPLACE GENERAL MOTORS?

WHICH FIRM WILL BECOME THE MODEL TO EMULATE FOR CORPORATIONS IN THE TWENTY-FIRST CENTURY? WHICH COMPANY WILL PROVIDE THE BLUEPRINT FOR CORPORATION V2.0?

Karim R. Lakhani

Alfred P. Sloan, president, CEO, and chairman of General Motors (GM) from the 1920s to 1950s, has been called the intellectual father of the modern American corporation. Sloan's genius was to invent the modern, multi-divisional firm—at its center were "smart" managers who made wise decisions about innovation, product development, manufacturing, marketing, and sales. Employees of the firm diligently followed managerial edicts and customers gladly bought their mass-manufactured and affordable automobiles. As a result, GM grew to be a global powerhouse. Unfortunately, Sloan's creation came to an official end when GM declared bankruptcy in 2009—signaling the end of Corporation v1.0.

So who will replace GM and be the model for v2.0? I would like to speculate that Threadless will feature as a likely candidate when future business historians begin to document the new models of the twenty-first-century corporation.

Central to the success and ethos of the "Threadless Way" is the recognition that its customers and users can participate in almost all aspects of the company's operations. Indeed, Threadless as a company collapses if its customers and users stop participating in the running of the firm. This is radical. Corporation v1.0 models its customers as passive consumers while Threadless invites them into its core operations. In creating Threadless, its founders enacted Friedrich von Hayek's insight from 1945 that knowledge in society is widely distributed and that no one organization can monopolize it. The Threadless model opens up the corporation so that distributed knowledge can flow through the organization as outsiders participate in the core functioning of the business.

This view of knowledge flow permeates all aspects of the Threadless business model. Take, for example, innovation and new product development. Success at innovation requires firms to be good at two important tasks: 1) Generating new, diverse ideas, and 2) Picking the best ideas for further development. Most firms hire a limited set of designers to generate the best ideas, and then executive management, through some Byzantine process, picks the best ideas (hopefully) to pursue. Threadless turns this model on its head, and instead embraces the notion of user-innovators as pioneered by Eric von Hippel, professor at the MIT Sloan School of Management. The key task of generating design ideas lies with the one million loyal customers, and in 2010

these users were submitting between 1,000 and 2,000 designs every week. Equally important, the second task of selection is also driven by Threadless users, who had, as of 2010, cast more than 133 million votes on the various designs. The Threadless model of user engagement shows how firms can completely reimagine the innovation process by being open to external knowledge flows.

Threadless has also discovered that its users not only want participation in the company, but also expect community interactions. Community at Threadless means affiliation, identification, and learning. Users want to meet other users, and want to interact with them. This interaction and exchange leads to a strong identification with others, and with Threadless. Community members interact for social connection around designs, while learning about new designs and approaches becomes the glue that holds the community together. The presence of a community also means that the center of gravity for decision-making shifts from internal managers to the community. Indeed, one can argue that Threadless is more of an online community that happens to have an interesting t-shirt store on the side, than an online t-shirt company with a quirky community on the side. Managing communities for innovation and profit is an art form that Threadless has pioneered, and this will provide important lessons for future scholars of management.

Since 2007, the Threadless business model has been taught to more than 2,000 MBA students and executives at the Harvard Business School, through the use of a multimedia business case study. Most participants come out energized and engaged about the possibilities of emulating the Threadless Way in a variety of diverse settings, including media, advertising, software development, and even automobiles. It is remarkable to reflect that major innovations in how to run the twenty-first-century corporation are likely to originate from a t-shirt company called Threadless.

Karim R. Lakhani is an assistant professor in the Technology and Operations Management Unit at the Harvard Business School. He specializes in the management of technological innovation and product development in firms and communities. He is coeditor of *Perspectives on Free and Open Source Software* (MIT Press, 2005), and co-founder of the MIT-based Open Source research community and web portal.

Funkalicious (opposite)
by **Christopher Golebiowski** aka **Fen**, Sweden
Score: 2.39/5 by 1,879 people

Breaking Up Is Hard to Do (above)
by **Leon Ryan** aka **d3d**, Australia
Score: 2.89/5 by 2,224 people

I wanted to show that living in a densely populated city can actually be part of a green lifestyle.

Stone Jungle

by **André da Silva Cruz** aka **acruz**, Brazil

Score: 3.07/5 by 2,181 people

Location: London, UK

Member since April 2003

I'm inspired by pop-culture nerdery. I care about the why of design a great deal more than the how. Stylistically my influences are Saul Bass, Paul Rand, Otl Aicher, government signage, Charlie Harper, and Optimus Prime.

Fame is my motivation (it's not going well). But really, I like to come up with ideas that make people laugh—to make them look at familiar objects in a different light. I'm always worried that my most recent good idea might be my last, so a lot of my motivation comes from trying to prove to myself that I can be consistent. Money is nice to have but creatively speaking I don't think anything good comes from chasing it. Do good work first and the money will come later.

Laziness is my technique. I try to spend more time thinking about each design than I do making it. As for the nitty-gritty, I mostly go straight into Illustrator. Pen rarely touches paper nowadays.

I wish I were better at photography. I've tried but I have no talent for it. I'd like to learn motion. It's a challenge for me, and a totally new way of thinking about design—but it will be worth it in the long run.

Regrets? None! Though I didn't go to art school and in some ways I wish I had. I'd probably be a lot better at typography, construction, and composition. On the other hand, I might not think about design in the same way that I do now.

I love Threadless. The feedback I got there taught me so much about design. It built my confidence, it paid my way through an English degree. ▶

OLLY MOSS *aka* WOSS

01

02

DIE HARD

ROBERT DE NIRO
THE DEER HUNTER

JOHN CAZALE · JOHN SAVAGE · MERYL STREEP · CHRISTOPHER WALKEN

Directed by MICHAEL CIMINO

03

04

Steven Spielberg's

**Indiana Jones
and the Last Crusade**

Videogame Classics 1998	Videogame Classics 2007	Videogame Classics 1999	Videogame Classics 1997
Metal Gear Solid	**Call of Duty 4: Modern Warfare**	**Silent Hill**	**GoldenEye**
Konami	**Infinity Ward**	**Konami**	Nintendo

Videogame Classics 2004	Videogame Classics 2008	Videogame Classics 1998	Videogame Classics 1998
The Sims 2	**Grand Theft Auto IV**	**Half-Life**	**The Legend of Zelda: The Ocarina of Time**
Maxis	**Rockstar**	**Valve**	Nintendo

I've always thought book cover design was the most interesting challenge—concept, image, and type all have to be considered. Until last year I'd always wanted to do a book cover for Penguin—and then I was lucky enough to be invited to pitch for one.

I get mistaken for Hugh Grant. But not nearly as often as I'd like. I do try so awfully hard.

Most of my work is done in bed with a laptop. I don't really have a life so it's mostly from the imagination. My surroundings make me want to stay inside and work more.

I still have the original *Consumable* creature (see page 8) and it has become my mascot. Although last year I had to surgically drain the juice out of him. It'd gone way past its expiry date. I was pretty young when I got my first print. Threadless gave me my start. My favorite work from other Threadless artists: *Moby Was a Consumer*, *Damn Scientists*, *Animals With Eyepatches! Yes!*, *Angels and Demons*. I'd also like to own *A Bigger Splash* by David Hockney.

What does my work offer to society? Absolutely nothing. Seriously, stop looking at it. Go and read a book or something. Not this book, a proper book.

01-03 **Films in Black and Red** (personal work)
04 **The Appleseed Cast** (gig poster)
05 **Videogame Classics** (personal work)

You can see some of Olly's Threadless designs on pages 8 (**08**), 45 (**05**), 69, 101 (**06**), 129 (**04**), and 170.

Type Tees allows people who are not designers to participate and submit ideas. When we first started the line, we worked with a bunch of different typography shops to set the slogans in appropriate typefaces. The type creators are credited on the site for their fonts. **Jake Nickell**

Meat Is Murder . . .

by **Stu** aka **Uts**, USA

Typeface **Tivoli** from **t26**

So Far . . .

by **Ariel Pascoe** aka **penguinsflyhi**, USA

Typeface **Tivoli** from **t26**

If You Can Read This . . .

by **Anthony Mihovich** aka **kamesen24**, USA

Typeface **Manifest Destiny** from **t26**

Procrastinators . . .

by **Brett Steelman** aka **twotwelve**, USA

Typeface **Tivoli** from **t26**

Stop Destroying . . .

by **Lawrence Pernica** aka **Larlar**, Canada

Typeface **Mr Mamoulian** from **t26**

95

Select

Let Our Veins Do the Talking (opposite)
by **Chuck Anderson**
aka **NoPattern**, USA

Select

The Motive (above)
by **Heiko Windisch**
aka **thestateofthings**, Germany

Select

01

I wanted to make the best poker shirt ever. So it was only natural to use the ace of spades, the highest card in the deck.

Poker Hand Values

by **Tan Nuyen** aka **Monkey II**, Netherlands

Score: 2.66/5 by 2,005 people

02

After a billion attempts, I finally tried to appeal to the Threadless community—but how? We're a such a varied group of nerds with weird, specific tastes. So I made a joke of it. It just seems so futile to classify our culture any more.

Music Snob

by **Spencer Fruhling**, Canada

Score: 2.67/5 by 2,166 people

03

Ballpoint pen through the wash, gone horribly right.

Splatter in D Minor

by **Joshuah Howard** aka **Jahoosawa**, USA

Score: 2.72/5 by 2,321 people

07

Love is complicated, but always worth it.

Puppet in Love

by **Lim Heng Swee** aka **ilovedoodle**, Malaysia

Score: 2.82/5 by 2,626 people

08

The shirt was inspired by an imagined trip taken by Marc Bolan of T. Rex to Montreal during Expo '67.

The Future Is Feeling

by **Neil Doshi** aka **futureface**, Canada

Select

09

This design was inspired by the treadmill I bought with the intention of losing some weight. But now this piece of equipment is just gathering dust in our house. Hehehe.

Runnin' Rhino

by **Allan Faustino** aka **alanis**, Philippines

Score: 3.14/5 by 2,200 people

13

Mmmm . . . sushi.

Mimi Henderlong aka **mimi**

The Last Piece

by **John Mitchell** aka **JOHN2**, USA

Score: 2.98/5 by 2,346 people

14

Sometimes you start out with a vague picture in your head, and the drawing goes in its own direction . . . and that direction sometimes ends up being a lion wearing glasses.

Lions Are Smarter Than I Am

by **Keith Carter** aka **keithmore**, USA

Score: 2.71/5 by 1,947 people

15

I was trying something simple—to make the fairies feel a bit sad.

The Good Guys Don't Glow at Midnight

by **Ivan Leonardo Vera Piñeros** aka **chippos**, Columbia

Score: 2.70/5 by 2,313 people

I'm sure there is an art history inside joke that I'm missing here, but bottom line: dude's got a sweet hairdo.

Dustin Henderlong aka **dhenderl**

Hadrian
by **Harsh Patel** aka **Cesar Suarez**, USA

Select

Routemaster bus—with a glamorous top-floor view.

Routemaster
by **Lehel Kovacs** aka **le_hell**, Hungary

Score: 2.87/5 by 2,284 people

A lot of people complained about this shirt, but I tried to make most of the references vague enough so that you'd need to have seen the movie to understand them. Well, except for "Snape Kills Dumbledore." Sorry! (PS: Harry kills Voldemort.)

Spoilt
by **Olly Moss** aka **Woss**, UK

Score: 3.41/5 by 2,176 people

10

This began as a joke with a crudely sketched skeletal face on a photo of a tee. It looked surprisingly cool so it then became a crudely vectored skeletal face on a photo of a tee. About fifteen minutes from initial idea to Threadless submission—easiest money I ever made!

Bone Idol
by **Stuart Colebrook** aka **Bramish**, Austria

Score: 2.24/5 by 2,248 people

A warning sign composed entirely of warning signs —the whole being the sum of its parts. The immediate association with danger is undermined by the playful nature of the iconography, and the situations the stick figures find themselves in.

Stick Figures in Peril
by **Brandt Botes** aka **vonbrandis**, South Africa

Score: 2.74/5 by 1,915 people

I didn't have this idea while eating Easter eggs (!!)—but I love this idea and love to imagine the baby's face!

A Birth Day
by **Jean-sébastien Deheeger** aka **nes-k**, France

Score: 3.10/5 by 2,445 people

When I was a kid I'd ride the spring ponies in the playground, and pretend to be a knight.

Playground Joust
by **Jillian Nickell** aka **jillustration**, USA

Score: 2.99/5 by 1,975 people

Three things cannot be long hidden: the sun, the moon, and the truth. And a black eye. Four, FOUR things.

Eclipse!
by **Ian Leino**, USA

Score: 2.87/5 by 2,838 people

I wanted to find out what Halloween would look like from this perspective. . . . What I discovered was haunting.

When I Was a Pumpkin
by **Josh Tuininga** aka **tuniguts**, USA

Score: 2.52/5 by 2,272 people

DESIGNS WITH A STORY

With the boring stuff out of the way, and our operations finally in order, in 2007 we were able to do amazing new things with Threadless. This was a year of transformations, endings, and exciting beginnings, and it wasn't always easy.

Probably the biggest change was in our printing methods. Before this year, we had strict color limits, design sizes, and placement specs. We decided to throw all that out. We allowed all-over printing, and offered up all kinds of colors, and crazy inks, like foils, UV, glow, and high-density. Designs had no limits. As you flip through this chapter, you'll begin to see tees that really push the bar when it comes to printing limitations. I kind of miss the days of all the simple, flat color, smaller prints, but we still do plenty of those, and now we have even more variety.

Another huge move was opening our first real, bricks-and-mortar store, in Chicago. We'd always wanted to, but always had trouble making a decision and pulling the trigger. Finally, we just said to ourselves, "A store would be awesome," and did it. Huge retailers

had been approaching us, wanting to carry our goods, but we kept saying no. We didn't feel as though the artist would be properly credited in the store. The tee would be just another tee on the shelves; the story wouldn't be there. We built our store to tell the stories behind the designs.

The Threadless store only carries the newest two weeks' worth of designs, and an LCD monitor displays information about each tee that is sold. We brought the interactive, community feeling of our website into the store in other ways. You can take a picture of yourself, and it will be shown in the shop window as though you are wearing one of the tees on display. Joe, our resident artist and snowboard superstar, also paints three display panels every week, based on the week's designs. My mind is blown by each and every one of them.

For the design submissions, we raised the prizing to $2,000 cash plus a $500 gift certificate if your design is printed. We also introduced a $500 reprint award for each time an artist's design is reprinted. All printed ▸

WE OFFERED UP ALL KINDS OF COLORS, AND CRAZY INKS, LIKE FOILS, UV, GLOW, AND HIGH-DENSITY

01 Our retail store brought Threadless into the real world. The monitors display live feed information about each tee.

02 Every artist who gets printed on Threadless receives a bona fide medal of honor, and induction into the Alumni Club.

03 Joe Suta creates three massive paintings a week for our store windows. The gas mask picture is the first one he painted.

01

artists became members of the Alumni Club, with access to a members-only forum, a t-shirt, coffee mug, mousepad, and—my personal favorite—a freaking medal of honor. The year saw our first licensing partnership with Blik wall graphics, too, so if an artist's design is chosen, and they agree to Blik using it, they score another $500.

We also decided to produce our own Threadless brand blank t-shirt. We spent a long time developing the perfect cut and moved all our printed designs over to our own-brand tees. Unfortunately, it turned out that few people cared about this. After some nightmares with our manufacturer, we are now moving away from our custom brand. But, boy, was that ever a learning experience.

Over the past few years, community members had been coming to the Threadless warehouse each September for a meet-up. This year we held our first official Threadless gathering, and called it the Family Reunion. Members from all around the world flew in to attend.

This is something we now do annually, and it grows every year. (I hope you attended the 2010 meet-up, and maybe got a free copy of this book. If not, shame on you: please come to next year's, say hi, and get some free stuff.)

We made a lot of changes on our website, such as adding an official critique section. We saw artists using the forum to ask for feedback on their designs, and the critique section provides a nice little venue for that to happen. Threadlesskids.com was launched, with designs for newborns to twelve-year-olds. This strangely coincided with the year my daughter was born. (Yay for Arli, love ya, sweetie!)

Shondi, my wife, had been working her butt off the past few years making sure we were doing all the things we were supposed to be doing as a real business. With Arli's birth imminent, and a completely unmanagable workload, she decided to start hiring an army of replacements and step down to become a full-time mommy.

01 Our office is in a constant state of flux. These desks lasted all of six months before we had to get rid of them in order to expand.

02 Shirts Our Business, one of our t-shirt printers, gave us this sweet custom scooter for a Christmas gift!

HARVARD BUSINESS SCHOOL DEVOTED AN ENTIRE CLASS TO STUDYING THREADLESS. TALK ABOUT HUMBLING

My partner, Jacob, also left Threadless in 2007. He had always been interested in the technical side of Threadless and became really engaged in emerging technologies, wanting to explore other possibilities. Like I said, endings as well as beginnings.

To close out the year, we decided to introduce a new annual awards ceremony called the Bestees. We gave out $100,000 in prizing for various categories, such as Designer of the Year, Most Printed, Groundbreaking Design, Collaborations, Newcomers, Kid-friendly, Best Use of Critique, Blogger of the Year, and Gallery Photo of the Year. This was such a fun thing to do, and continues to be something to look forward to at the end of the year on Threadless.

Oh, and did I mention that Harvard Business School did a case study on our business model? An entire class was devoted to studying Threadless. They came and shot a bunch of videos and interviews, setting up a full curriculum around our business. Talk about humbling.

In 2007, a super-talented, multi-printed Threadless designer by the name of Jublin placed our millionth order. We saw previously huge Threadless artists, such as Glennz, move on to do their own thing, and new blood rising to the top. While it's easy to get nostalgic about things, it's just as easy (and much more useful) to be excited for what's to come.

Biggie Was Right (opposite)

by **Graham Shephard** aka **Tonteau**, UK

Score: 2.14/5 by 2,146 people

Beat It (above)

by **Adam White** aka **adamwhite**, USA

Score: 2.16/5 by 2,462 people

We took our Type Tees line to the next level by moving away from simple type on t-shirts to creating a unique illustration that complements each slogan. **Jake Nickell**

Movies . . .

by **Jayson Dougherty** aka **ZombieToArt**, Australia

Typeface **Brown Black** by **ShinnType**

Nerds . . .

by **Chris Broll** aka **chisafer**, USA

Typeface **Kanal Regular** by **Identikal** from **t26**

I Listen to Bands . . .

by **Evan Ferstenfeld** aka **FRICKINAWESOME**, USA

Typeface **Brown Bold** by **ShinnType**

Video Games

by **Lawrence Pernica** aka **Larlar**, Canada

Typeface **Kanal Regular** by **Bit Kit** from **t26**

Being Vague . . .

by **Steve Wierth** aka **Torakamikaze**, USA

Typeface **Walburn** by **ShinnType**

My style now tends to lean toward *geometric abstractionism*, but at the time I created Hairwolves *and* Clouds Within the Thunder, *I was really trying to push my drawing skills. My birthday present that year, a Wacom Tablet, made it much easier to learn. Thanks, Mom and Dad.*

Hairwolves (opposite)

by **Joe Van Wetering** aka **speedyjvw**, USA

Score: 2.64/5 by 2,016 people

Clouds Within the Thunder (above)

by **Joe Van Wetering** aka **speedyjvw**, USA

Score: 2.56/5 by 2,476 people

actions and inventions come first

LANGUAGE FOLLOWS IN THEIR WAKE. WORDS, HOWEVER DIFFERENT THEIR MEANINGS, ALL CAME INTO INTO EXISTENCE FOR THE SAME REASON: PEOPLE GET TIRED OF SAYING, "YOU *KNOW* . . . THAT *THING*."

Jeff Howe

I spent the first half of 2005 watching a certain set of actions and inventions, and found myself at a loss to describe them. I was following the Vans Warped Tour[01] for a story. The kids on the tour were prodigiously and promiscuously creative. They made poetry, and videos, and animations, and tattoos, and all manner of designs. They weren't doing it for money or because they'd received a memo telling them to do these things. And they didn't want to become a filmmaker, or a poet. They were making stuff because, as we all know very well in our heart of hearts, making stuff—and let me stop at this point to emphasize that "stuff" is meant here to be interpreted as broadly as possible, so as to include a hand-tied steel-head fly, a straw that contains its own water filter,[02] and the mix tapes you made your eighth grade girlfriend[03]—making stuff is the most joyful occupation in which we ever engage. It is, as any theologian worth his or her salt will cheerfully concede, the closest we come to God.

And we all know this, right? For thousands of years we're all going into our garages or stone outhouses or huts and making stuff when we're not planting crops, or hunting, or battling off Visigoths, or some shit. And for thousands of years that stuff got put up on a shelf, or buried with its maker, or just maybe it got sold on market day to bring in an extra farthing or two. But mostly it got shunted aside; it became a form of economic and cultural dark matter—it possessed a powerful gravitational pull, but it was nearly impossible to measure. And because humans are primitive creatures, and our tools of measurement and analysis are blunt and imprecise, we all made the mistake of dividing our lives into "work" and all that other stuff that we called "hobbies." It was a false dichotomy; it created an imbalance, and we should have known that one day a reckoning would come.

Which brings me back to 2005, and the Vans Warped Tour, and the reckoning, because that's what I saw in these kids. Massive, historical forces were shifting into a new alignment. What previous generations of humans called the hobby were achieving ascendancy over what said predecessors called work. Weird. Scary. True. And what does one call *that*? I called it crowdsourcing, and wrote about the phenomenon first in *Wired* magazine in June 2006, and then in a book that followed a few years later. But the word is far less interesting than the thing it attempts to name.

And now here's where Threadless comes in, because Jake, and Jake, and Jeffrey, and company were hip to this historical realignment eons ago, and they built a company that would be all about taking the wonderful, crazy, hysterically funny, bizarre, offensive, eccentric stuff that people make, and pulling it out of the garage, and the hut, and the upstairs shelf, and introducing it to anyone and everyone with an Internet connection.

It's not surprising that people gravitated to Threadless. Because, really, they were gravitating to one another. The genius of Threadless (and they're not alone) is that they put the community on a pedestal, and then stepped into the background. It takes a special company to understand that their ego—their creativity, their brilliance, their ideas—are welcome, but not necessary. What's necessary is to be the room in which the party takes place. And so Threadless became an impeccable host.

When Jake Nickell asked me to write this essay he suggested speculating on the future of crowdsourcing. What I *want* to say is that it'll look a lot like Threadless: people sharing their lovely (and nasty) creations with each other and the rest of the world in a forum that values such creative expressions. But I don't think that it *will* look a lot like that.

What happened is that a lot of businesses looked at a company like Threadless and noticed one thing: cheap labor. That misses the point, of course, but this won't stop a slough of soulless companies from proliferating. So be it. I—we—have a big consolation. Whatever happens, somewhere out there is another crew like Jake, and Jake, and Jeffrey just waiting to start everything fresh again. We won't know what to call that either, but I for one won't mind that one bit.

footnotes
01 A movable punk rock feast. An endurance marathon punk rock festival that's as much about the fans as it is the bands.
02 A real thing: A Danish inventor created the LifeStraw to help eradicate waterborne diseases in nations without access to clean drinking water.
03 Run don't walk to cassettefrommyex.com.

Jeff Howe coined the term "crowdsourcing" in an influential essay in 2006 for *Wired* magazine, where he is a contributing editor. He has continued to cover the phenomenon in his blog, crowdsourcing.com, and published a book on the subject in 2008 for Crown Books. Jeff has also been a senior editor at inside.com and a writer at the *Village Voice*. He has written for *Time* magazine, the *Washington Post*, and numerous other publications. He lives in Brooklyn.

FOOD WITH FACES

I never would have predicted the Food with Faces trend! Who would've thought that so many designs that make characters out of stuff we eat would end up so popular? I guess people like to play with their food, or maybe for their food to play? **Jake Nickell**

Inside You

by **Matt Palmer** aka **bananaphone**, Australia

Score: 2.54/5 by 2,936 people

There's No Crying in Breakfast

by **Philip Tseng** aka **pilihp**, USA

Score: 3.00/5 by 2,559 people

Refrigerator Running

by **Josh Perkins** aka **theperk**, USA

Score: 2.88/5 by 2,429 people

You Really Grate on Me

by **Gemma Correll** aka **gemmabear**, UK

Score: 3.28/5 by 1,148 people

Bad Apple

by **Tan Nuyen** aka **Monkey III**, Netherlands

Score: 2.52/5 by 2,377 people

Location: Kuala Lumpur, Malaysia

Member since January 2007

I enjoy creating something we can't see in our real life. People like surprises, something they've never seen. The easiest way to "wow" people is through the imagination.

For about a year I could say that submitting t-shirts to Threadless was my full-time job. One of the main reasons was because of the Flying Mouse 365 (FM365) project, which started in February 2009. I rejected all job offers because of it. I'd decided to submit a t-shirt design to Threadless every day of the year.

The most challenging part of FM365 was that I had to think of the idea and also draw it in the same day. But that working method wasted a lot of time, and it was tough to come up with a great idea every day. After three months finally I decided to stop drawing for a while and put all my time into the ideas. I spent six weeks, and came up with about 300 ideas in my sketchbook. Then all I had to do was the drawing part.

Designs that need a few paragraphs of explanation don't work on Threadless. The Threadless community is special, they want something clear and easy to get. So I always try to let the design speak for itself.

I have to say thank you to the "Threadless God." Also to the Threadless community for its recognition. I'm really happy to be the most printed designer on Threadless—I never thought I could go that far, and now I've been able to make t-shirt design my career. ▸

CHOW HON LAM *a.k.a.* **FLYING MOUSE**

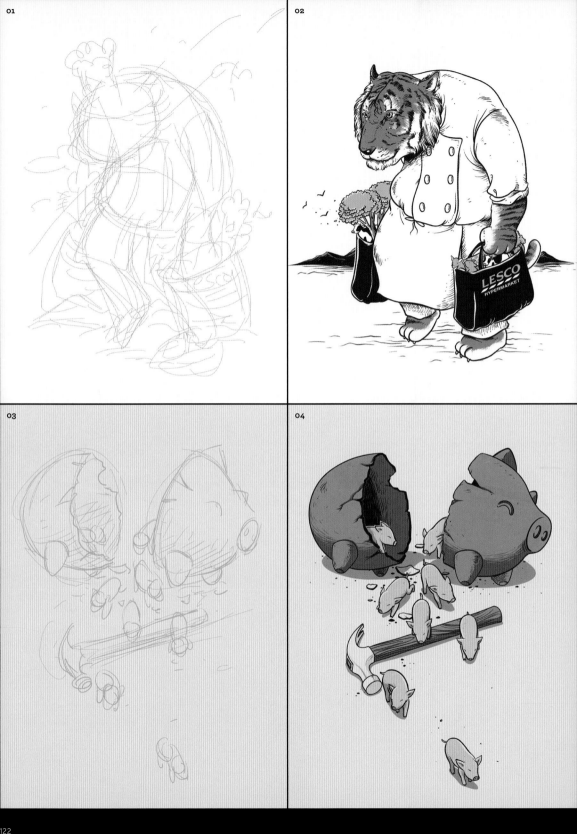

Though I liked drawing I didn't have a chance to go to art school. My first art-related job was as a part-time FA artist, or DTP operator, in a small design house. Then I started getting some freelance work—illustration, children's book design, manga, character designs, coloring work—and published my own manga in 1998. I wrote the story, drew the pages, and found a printer and distributor. Then in 2007, I found Threadless.

When I was nominated for Martell's Rising Personalities Award 2009 the judging panel was just like what we always see in reality TV shows. It was fun, actually. It was a really new experience for me—the photo shoots, video interviews, newspaper interviews. I came to their attention because of Threadless. The finalists were all from different media industries—DJ, jewelry designer, TV host, artist....

Among other designs on Threadless, I like *Poker Hand Values* by Tan Nuyen. I really like the flock printing on that shirt—it's classy.

I hope my work can bring people a smile.

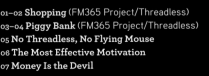

You can see more of Chow's Threadless designs on pages 128 (**07**) and 161 (**11**).

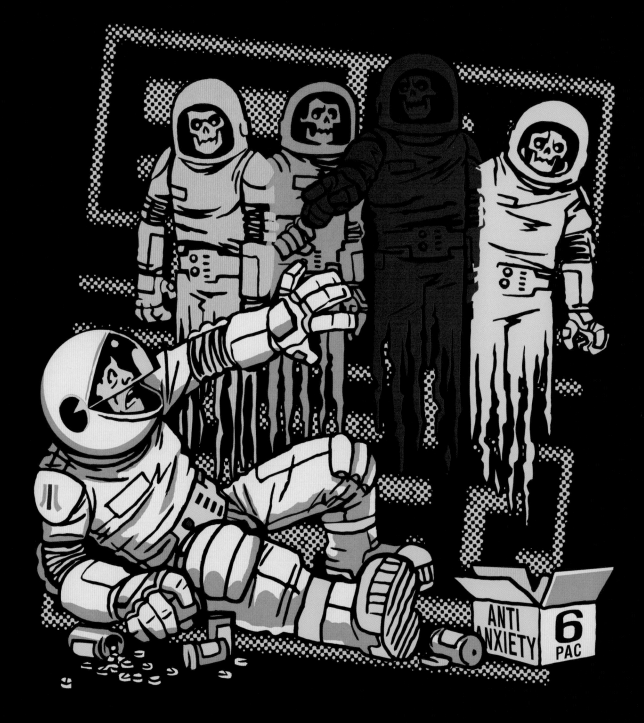

The Madness of Mission 6 (opposite)

by **Travis Pitts** aka **travis76**, USA

Score: 2.61/5 by 2,382 people

Color-Coded Criminals (above)

by **Loy Valera** aka **kaloyster**, Philippines

Score: 3.29/5 by 2,517 people

125

2008

01

With this design, I wanted to focus on the idea of positive and negative space as well as the notion of duality within an image. I also really wanted a design printed on fuchsia.

And How Are You Feeling Today?

by **Jan Avendano** aka **funkie fresh**, Canada

Score: 2.26/5 by 1,884 people

02

Liberty is inspired by my childhood memories from my hometown in San Isidro, Nueva Ecija, about little folk tales woven by old aunts who have nothing else to do aside from knitting kitchen pot-holders.

Liberty

by **Kneil Melicano** aka **roadkill3d**, Philippines

Score: 3.24/5 by 2,069 people

03

I wanted to do a music-inspired piece featuring an LP. Then it occurred to me that I could connect the lines on the record with the pinstripes on a suit, and voilà, *Music Business* was born!

Music Business Remastered

by **Dale Edwin Murray** aka **DaleEdwin**, UK

Score: 2.94/5 by 1,258 people

07

The black cat—her eyes, her expression, and her elegant movements—has a powerful air of mystery. I always think a black cat is going to do something surreal. Next time you're at the beach, see if one is around.

I Got Another Whale

by **Chow Hon Lam** aka **Flying Mouse**, Malaysia

Score: 2.39/5 by 1,929 people

08

While illustrating *Word!* all I could think about was one time I visited the library and all the characters from all of your favorite books were having the nastiest, geekiest sex imaginable.

Word!

by **Matt Palmer** aka **bananaphone**, Australia

Score: 2.64/5 by 1,888 people

09

A huge angry ape throwing barrels from the top of a construction site: the premise for one of the most popular video games of all time. I thought the idea of this being an occupational hazard for everyday construction workers was pretty funny. The community at Threadless was instrumental in developing this design in the critique section—it was a real team effort!

Occupational Hazard

by **Aled Lewis** aka **fatheed**, UK

Score: 3.20/5 by 1,390 people

13

In his downtime, Mr. Roboto likes to go sightseeing and explore the city.

Mr. Roboto Goes Sightseeing

by **Philip Tseng** aka **pilihp**, USA

Score: 2.83/5 by 1,242 people

14

Ultra-violent thieves vs. DIY kits: a match made in heaven.

Clockwork Kit

by **Kerkko Ulmanen** aka **gummi**, Finland

Score: 2.59/5 by 2,012 people

15

A simple visual of a familiar saying.

Birds of a Feather

by **Ross Zietz** aka **arzie13**, USA

Score: 3.40/5 by 1,602 people

A silly response to the popular *Keep Calm and Carry On* poster. Designed during the recession, when keeping calm was the last thing on most people's minds.

Now Panic and Freak Out

by **Olly Moss** aka **Woss**, UK

Type Tees

Just think lovely, wonderful, happy thoughts. And up you go!

I'm Like a Bird!

by **Lim Heng Swee**
aka **ilovedoodle**, Malaysia

Score: 3.61/5 by 1,173 people

Bye Bye Apocalypse is about leaving all your worries behind. Although the bigger picture is obviously terrifying, there are always fun memories.

Bye Bye Apocalypse

by **Budi Satria Kwan** aka **radiomode**, Singapore

Score: 3.27/5 by 1,166 people

I originally thought up this design for a local arts conference called Spark. Some Thread-pals encouraged me to sub it to Threadless instead, which ended up being a great decision.

Graphite for Your Right

by **David Creighton-Pester**
aka **WanderingBert**, New Zealand

Score: 2.54/5 by 1,723 people

11

Keep It Simple Stupid may have been a by-product of working for a bike company or of my love of Rube Goldberg–esque contraptions, or both. Either way, there's nothing more conceptual behind it than aiming to create the most absurdly complex vintage bicycle conceivable.

Keep It Simple Stupid

by **Aaron Hogg** aka **hogboy**, New Zealand

Score: 3.05/5 by 1,186 people

Nature's most epic battle. This design is taken from an ink and brush drawing that I did.

The Squid vs. the Whale

by **Brandon Ancone**
aka **Bancone Illustration**, USA

Score: 2.97/5 by 1,278 people

This design is a union of my passions for pop art, retro stuff, colors, and experimentation.

Colorblind

by **Matheus Lopes** aka **mathiole**, Brazil

Score: 3.64/5 by 1,896 people

I love the exclamation point in the title. It needs to be yelled for full effect. Preferably over a thumping bassline.

Bob Nanna aka **BNannas**

Egyptronic!

by **Elise Nishiyama**
aka **SayonaraGangster**, USA

Score: 1.89/5 by 2,156 people

Darkness is only a curtain, waiting to be unfolded.

Hey, Mr. Blue Sky

by **Lim Heng Swee**
aka **ilovedoodle**, Malaysia

Score: 3.42/5 by 1,871 people

A PERFECT LITTLE COMMUNITY

One of the most important things about running Threadless is balancing the business side with the fun-loving, amazing, creative community side. When you're at work, and feeling you should be doing something productive, it's easy to get caught up in the operations of selling and shipping t-shirts. Truth is, browsing the blogs, voting on tees, and keeping up with the community is just as important—and way more fun! In 2008 we started to feel as though we were working too hard on some things and not playing hard enough with the thousands of friends who interact with Threadless every day.

We decided to make it part of people's jobs to spend time involved with our community. Charlie and Craig, who had both been working with Threadless for many years, began to take on these roles. Charlie started putting on a lot of exciting things for the community, like Threadlemanss—a Pinewood Derby event that took place in our office. If you were ever in Cub Scouts, you know that the Pinewood Derby is a model car racing event where you carve your vehicle out of a block of wood using a standard kit, paint it, and race it against the cars built by other scouts. We held a global, multi-day derby where artists and companies around the world sent in cars, and we raced them all.

Craig set up Threadless Tee-V. He had been filming random hijinks around the office since back in 2004, and posting them on his personal website. With Threadless Tee-V, he was able to post those videos officially on Threadless, and start recording new material, such as interviews with all the bands that come through our office, weekly updates on Threadless, and promotional videos. It's a great way for us to show all the random awesomeness that is taking place in Threadlessland.

To take care of our artist liaison, we hired Mimi. She is the single point of contact for all artists to communicate with Threadless about their designs. ▸

01

WE WERE WORKING TOO HARD AND NOT PLAYING HARD ENOUGH WITH FRIENDS ON THREADLESS

02

01 Our yearly tradition of "wear your ugly Christmas sweater to work day" in full swing.

02 A shot from Threadless Kids, which opened in Chicago. Threadless IRL part two.

01

02

I WANTED TO GET BACK TO UNDERSTANDING, GROWING, AND INTERACTING WITH THE THREADLESS COMMUNITY

Before Mimi, that side of things was pretty haphazard: instant messaging conversations with our production staff, emails to five or six different people, who didn't always pass on every little detail to each other. Mimi was also tasked with setting up new programs for Threadless artists (more about that in 2009).

We took the meet-up this year to a whole new level, with plenty of things to do, and free food, beer, and tees of course. We make a huge effort with the Family Reunions, and they just keep getting better and better. There are also Threadless meet-ups throughout the year and around the world.

After the success of our Threadless store, we decided to do the same for our Kids line, and opened up in the Wicker Park neighborhood of Chicago (one piece of advice: Never open a t-shirt store in the dead of winter!). On the website side of things, we decided to separate two of our other t-shirt lines, Select and Type Tees, into their own websites. The splitting of the sites allowed the stories of those brands to be told individually, and for the scoring and submitting community of Type Tees to exist on its own site.

The Bestee awards, first introduced in 2007, were rebooted this year with the People's Choice—the design of the year chosen by the community, and with a prize worth $20,000! We also launched a line of art prints, where we screen-printed t-shirt designs on to high-quality paper. My favorite thing was that we worked with a bunch of small, local screen-printing shops in Chicago to do the printing.

During this time of refocusing back on our community, I also felt that I personally was spending too much time on the operations of the business, and wanted to get back to understanding, growing, and interacting with the Threadless community. At the same time, I was planning to move my family to Colorado, and set up a small satellite office there. After considering the options, I decided it would be best to step down as chief executive, and hire a CEO to run Threadless while I shifted positions and made my move.

The search didn't take long. Tom comes from the music industry—his start-up, Cductive, which was eventually bought by eMusic, sold MP3s on the Internet for $0.99 back in 1999. Groundbreaking stuff!

We felt he was a really great fit—especially as he had been working with artists (musicians) for a while. He's a super-smart dude with a very entrepreneurial, scrappy work style. Tom began early in the year, so we had a chance to work together for quite some time before I relocated in the late summer. We have a small office in Boulder, which includes Dustin, our event coordinator, and Mimi. We've created a perfect little community zone out here.

04

01 Charlie Festa was able to score us this neon sign for a mere $500.

02 Another new tradition—pumpkin carving by Craig Shimala!

03 Here's our Boulder office. Our sign lasted about an hour before our landlord came knocking. Ha.

04 Uh, what? Most Innovative Small Company in America? Whoa!

Braaains! (opposite)

by **Ray Frenden**, USA

Score: 2.5/5 by 1,807 people

Yes or No? (above)

by **Ericka Gonzalez** aka **Ericka_Gonzalez**, USA

Score: 2.52/5 by 1,149 people

A RABBIT NEVER WOULD HAVE WORKED, BRO

How would you describe the Dick Firestorm style? And how is *THE LAST F*CKIN'* *UNICORN* **a consummate Dick Firestorm piece?** BRO, THE DICK FIRESTORM STYLE CAN BE BEST DESCRIBED AS "TOTALLY FUCKIN' BADASS." ALL MY DESIGNS ARE PRETTY MUCH MADE UP OF THE SAME FOUR ELEMENTS: DEATH, DESTRUCTION, FIREBALLS, AND TITTIES. BUT BRO, THE REAL REASON THAT *THE LAST FUCKIN' UNICORN* IS A SUCCESS IS 'CAUSE I GOT SAM SCHUNA TO DRAW IT. **Why a unicorn? Did you try using any other adorable animal instead of a unicorn? Could this have been** *The Last Bunny Rabbit*? I ALWAYS FUCKIN' HATED UNICORNS. A RABBIT NEVER WOULD HAVE WORKED, BRO. LISTEN, IF YOU'RE GONNA BE SCORCHIN' ONE OF GOD'S CREATURES FOR A METAL DESIGN, THEN YOU GOTTA MAKE SURE YOU'RE SCORCHIN' SOMETHIN' THAT'S MAGICAL, MAJESTIC, AND ENDANGERED. **What music were you listening to when you came up with this?** I REMEMBER BEIN' AT A BAR HAVIN' A PRETTY SOLID TIME WHEN SOME DUMBASS WENT UP TO THE JUKEBOX AND PUT ON THAT "DANCING QUEEN" SONG BY THOSE ABBA ASSCLOWNS. BRO, AS SOON AS I HEARD THE FIRST FEW NOTES, ALL I COULD THINK ABOUT WAS WANTING TO DESTROY THINGS WITH FIRE. THAT WAS THE GENESIS OF THE UNICORN DESIGN. **You've collaborated with Sam Schuna (aka olie!) and Aled Lewis (aka Fatheed). Is there a collaboration with your friend Kenny in the future? Perhaps for the surprise lovechild of** *THE LAST F*CKIN' UNICORN*? THE LAST TIME ME AND KENNY SAT DOWN WITH THE INTENTION OF FLESHING OUT A DESIGN TOGETHER, WE ENDED UP GETTIN' SMASHED ON CHEAP MEXICAN BEERS, AND TAKEN TO THE POLICE STATION FOR TRYIN' TO SET A FIRE INSIDE BED AND BATH AND BEYOND. I DON'T KNOW WHEN OUR COLLAB IS GONNA HAPPEN, BUT WHEN IT FINALLY DOES, IT'S GONNA BE ONE FOR THE RECORD BOOKS. **You're from the great Garden State, would you care to reveal which city?** I AIN'T GONNA REVEAL A CITY. YOU KNOW WHY, BRO? 'CAUSE THE WHOLE FUCKIN' STATE OF NEW JERSEY IS DICK FIRESTORM'S TURF. I'M LIKE A WILD FIRE, BRO. I CAN'T BE CONTAINED IN ONE SMALL AREA. **Will you ever release your sketchbook post mortem? It would be a goldmine of awesomeness.** BRO, IF THE AVERAGE PERSON LOOKED AT JUST ONE PAGE OF MY SKETCHBOOK, THEIR FACE WOULD MELT OFF LIKE WHEN THEY OPENED UP THAT BOX IN THE FIRST *INDIANA JONES*. THE GENERAL PUBLIC COULDN'T HANDLE THE KIND OF WILD SHIT THAT I DRAW IN THERE. TRUST ME, BRO. **This book gives you a chance to become a legend. How does that feel?** IT FEELS PRETTY FUCKIN' SOLID. PEOPLE HEAR ABOUT ME ON THE SIX O'CLOCK NEWS ALL THE TIME, BUT I NEVER THOUGHT THEY'D READ ABOUT ME IN AN ART BOOK. DICK FIRESTORM IS GONNA BE A HOUSEHOLD NAME SOMEDAY AND IT'S ALL BECAUSE OF THREADLESS. **Any words you'd like to say in honor of Threadless's ten-year anniversary?** THREADLESS MAKES PEOPLE'S DREAMS COME TRUE AND SHIT. CONGRATULATIONS ON TEN KILLER YEARS.

THE LAST F*CKIN' UNICORN

by **Dick Firestorm** and **Sam Schuna**
aka **dick firestorm** and **olie!**, USA

Score: 2.57/5 by 1,604 people

LOVES TEES

These tees represent winners of various Loves competitions, which are design challenges based around a theme—such as Revolution or True Stories. The thing I love most about these is that they're not branded despite being the result of a partnership with other companies and organizations; they just use the themes as inspiration. **Jake Nickell**

Elephas Maximus (Good)

by **Thomas De Santis** aka **Montro**, Dominican Republic

Score: 3.43/5 by 1,848 people

Squeegee Clean (Revolution)

by **Reilly Stroope**, USA

Score: 3.46/5 by 1,827 people

Animals with Eyepatches! Yes! (Lollapalooza)

by **Brock Davis** aka **Laser Bread**, USA

Score: 2.64/5 by 1,660 people

Judith + Holofernes (True Stories)

by **Frank Barbara** aka **franx**, Canada

Score: 3.03/5 by 1,111 people

Piggy Board (Human Giant)

by **Preston Haynes** aka **Merboy**, USA

Score: 2.13/5 by 1,829 people

THREADLESS IS A PERFECT EXAMPLE OF (ARTONOMICS)

John Maeda

IT ISN'T SIMPLY AN ONLINE STORE. IT'S THE IDEAL MIX OF AN AUTHENTIC EXPRESSION OF ARTISTIC PRACTICE WITH INNOVATIVE ECONOMIC MODELS.

Launching a web-based company back in 2000, just when the dot-com bubble burst and many e-tailers were struggling, was risky business. But that's what the guys at Threadless did, and they've not only survived, they've flourished.

In December 2008, Dustin Hostetler (Select curator at Threadless) invited me to participate in the company's first guest-curated Threadless Select series by hand-picking a collection of shirts designed by members of the Rhode Island School of Design [RISD] community. When I first met Dustin, I got a sense of how he came to be an artist-entrepreneur, and realized that his story sounded strangely similar to those of the RISD grads I talk to every day. The common thread I have found in these conversations is that for many creative people, the idea of actually earning money for what they do reeks of "selling out." Some consciously choose to be "starving artists" devoted solely to making their own work, unconcerned about whether or not the world eventually "discovers" them. Others choose a more entrepreneurial route by creating designs and making art with a greater sensitivity to the market.

And then there are those who choose to do both— who vary the emphasis between more commercial and non-commercial creative pursuits during the course of their lives.

I believe that as the world continues to struggle with monumental challenges—challenges that require our most creative thinkers to find inspired solutions—it is essential to push the notion of artists-as-entrepreneurs one step further. Artists, designers, and other creative types need to become leaders, like those at Threadless. Our best "artrepreneurs" also have the ability to lead and inspire others. This lies at the heart of what I call The RISD IDEA (Intuition, Design, Emotion, Art). I use this acronym because I see it as a necessary complement to another widely used term in today's world: STEM (Science, Technology, Engineering, Math). Recently, the US government, and many others throughout the world, have been touting STEM as the be-all-and-end-all to innovation. But in the 2010s, I expect more people will begin to realize that it is a synthesis of both STEM and IDEA that will lead to true innovation.

Threadless is a success because it realizes the power of a creative network rather than a strict organizational hierarchy. In the rush to develop ever newer and "better" products, "better" has too often meant "more technology." As we struggle to make sense of the "progress" and possibilities that all of this technology can bring, we need to acknowledge artists' and designers' power to make technology understandable, to make sense of information overload, and to use their intuitive sense to appeal to others' true emotions. Making people feel something—feel better—is where real progress comes from. I see this every day at RISD, and am pleased to see that the creative leaders at Threadless clearly see it, too.

John Maeda, president of Rhode Island School of Design, is a world-renowned artist, designer, computer scientist, and educator. At RISD, he seeks to champion the necessary role that artists and designers play in the creative economy. His work is in the permanent collections of the Museum of Modern Art (MoMA), the San Francisco Museum of Modern Art, and the Cartier Foundation in Paris. John's most recent book, *The Laws of Simplicity*, is an international bestseller. In 2008, he was named by *Esquire* magazine as one of the 75 most influential individuals of the twenty-first century.

Shredded A (above)

by **Brock Davis**
aka **Laser Bread**, USA

Score: 3.39/5 by 1,228 people

When Pandas Attack (opposite)

by **Jimi Benedict** and **A.J. Dimarucot**
aka **jimiyo vs. aj dimarucot**, USA/Philippines

Score: 3.06/5 by 1,335 people

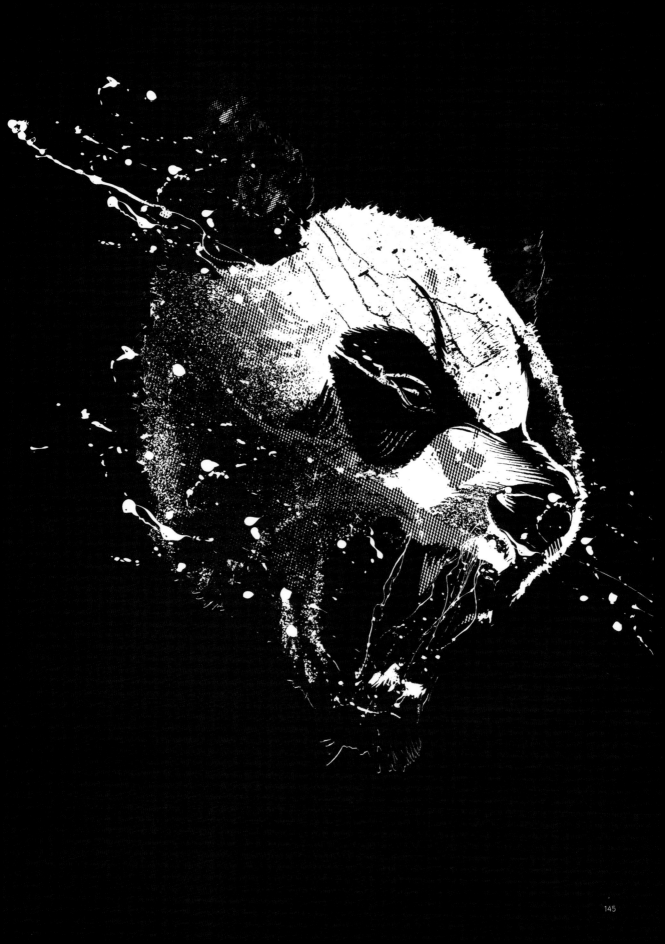

YOU CAN TAKE IT WITH YOU

I was on my way to Bulgaria for a breakdancing competition, and was really missing my daughter, wife, and everything back home. I wanted to bring them all with me. I was thinking about birds migrating and having to leave everything behind, but what if there was a bird who could take everything on its journey? *Bird Migration* is special to me. It was my first printed Threadless design and it won a Loves Tees design challenge (the theme was Travel). The prize was a trip to the incredible country of Iceland (*above*), and the band Calexico even wrote a song called *Absent Afternoon* inspired by the design! *Bird Migration* brought fire back into my artwork, as well as the inspiration and motivation that I needed at the time. **Alex Solis**

Bird Migration (opposite)

by **Alex Solis** aka **alexmdc**, USA

Score: 3.54/5 by 1,332 people

Location: London, UK

Member since June 2006

For two years before my graphic design degree I worked in a customer call center. I did learn a great deal about mortgages, but it was a soul-crushing, dead-end job.

My only real creative output at that time was painting. I had some of my work in a local gallery, but the bulk of my paintings were sold through eBay. I was always reluctant to put a price on my work, so the self-regulating process of bidding made that aspect a lot easier. Plus, who doesn't enjoy the thrill of an auction!

A friend introduced me to Threadless in the summer of 2006 at the Isle of Wight Festival. He was wearing a Glennz tee, *Go Japan!*, that I thought was completely awesome. I signed up that week and started submitting designs shortly after. I have something of an addictive personality, and Threadless pretty quickly became my new addiction.

What seems to surprise a lot of people is that I hand-draw my designs. I've tried different approaches, including photography, typography, infographic, and straight-up Illustrator work, but the style that has emerged for me over the past two years is line drawing illustration. Pencil and ink drawing is second nature to me and it has proven hard to give up.

Most of my work begins life as a doodle in one of my sketchbooks. I have a bunch on the go at any one time, and I almost always have a sketchbook on me whenever I go out. ▸

ALED LEWIS *aka* FATHEED

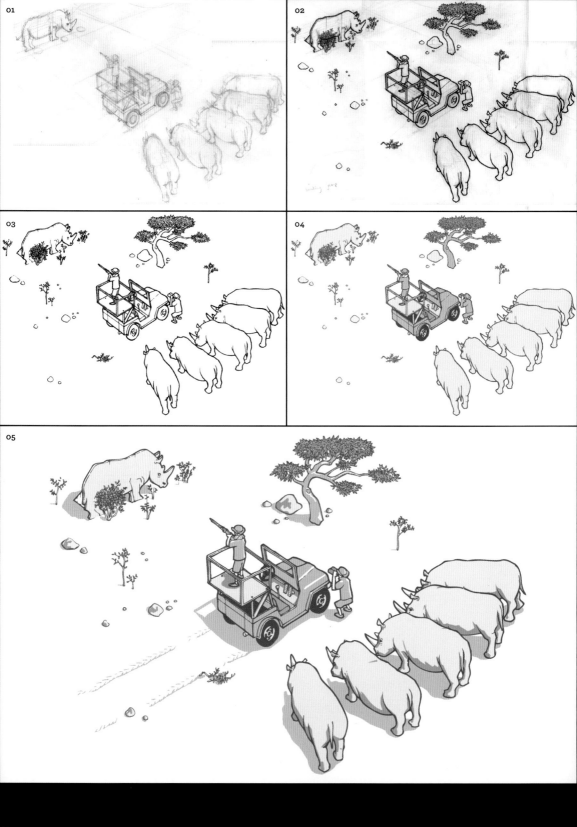

that make me laugh or get my attention in everyday s... ons sometimes translate well into silly design ideas in my head. I heard it said once that the classic comedy formula involves placing an ordinary thing in an extraordinary situation, or placing an extraordinary thing in an ordinary situation, and this principle has always worked for me.

Working on Threadless has focused the way that I think about visual communication. It is one thing to come up with an interesting or funny concept, but it is another to condense a complex narrative into a single concise scene.

I've learned how to use line thickness to give importance to some elements over others and allow a sense of perspective in an illustration. The first stage is to pencil the sketch, then to ink the lines. I scan and edit it in Photoshop and vector the lines in Illustrator. This gives the illustration really crisp edges, which is ideal for screen-printing, but keeps the variations in line thickness that give it a hand-drawn feel.

Most of my design work is done at my computer desk, which at this moment doubles as my bedside table. It's not ideal—especially if I'm working late into the night. Thankfully I have a very patient girlfriend. The dream is to have a big studio space with lots of desks, and drawers, and inspiring visual stuff. Living in London means a humble living space.

Funkalicious is an awesome design. No words can adequately describe why it's so cool, but everyone knows that it is. I love the older Type Tees. There are some real classic ones with simple, clever messages presented as unfussy, elegant typographic designs. *Allow Me To Explain Through Interpretive Dance*, and *Procrastinators: The Leaders of Tomorrow* are the two that get washed the most, and I don't think a shirt has ever been more relevant to me than the second one.

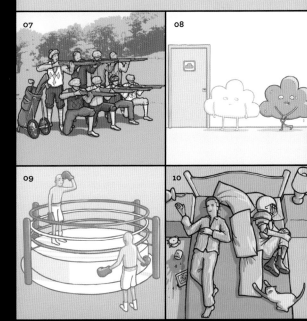

01–05 **Rhinos Hunt in Packs** (Threadless)
06 **Foam Monster in Emotional Reunion with Severed Limb** (Threadless)
07–10 Illustrations for Reader's Digest Asia

You can see more of Aled's Threadless designs on pages 128 (09), 175 and 205.

Boynado (opposite)
by **Brock Davis** aka **Laser Bread**, USA
Score: 3.36/5 by 1,096 people

Playin' in the Sprinkler (above)
by **Jason Bergsieker** aka **NomadSlim**, USA
Score: 3.24/5 by 1,147 people

2008 PEOPLE'S CHOICE

Mr. Melicano, this shirt is perfection.
Fierce, realistic wolf pelt? Check.
Sexy pout? Check.
Sideswept bangs and mysteriously hidden eyes? Check.
Houndstooth print? Check.
Cute but deadly weapon? Check.
Gingham and wicker? Check.
Independent woman? Check.
Glorious coloring, shading, and lines? Check.
Grimm's fairy tale reference? Check.
Zena Hardt aka **sniima**

RED
by **Kneil Melicano** aka **roadkill3d**, Philippines

Score: 3.51 by 1,281 people

2009

01

The original gym rat!

Let's Get Physical
by **Keith Kuniyuki** aka **herky**, USA

Score: 3.31/5 by 813 people

02

I knew I wanted to do something with geometric shapes, astronauts, and maybe type. Somehow in the crazy blender of my brain the idea formed to do a parody of the classic *Clockwork Orange* poster with the rocket pop replacing the switchblade.

Freakanaut
by **Aaron Hogg** aka **Style Swap**, New Zealand

Score: 2.86/5 by 755 people

03

We're total night owls and often stay up late working on our illustrations, which seems to be common among artists. The "night gardener" is a visual metaphor for this, creating his work while the rest of the world sleeps.

The Night Gardener
by **Terry Fan** and **Eric Fan**
aka **igo2cairo** and **opifan64**, Canada

Score: 3.70/5 by 784 people

07

I don't like coffee in the morning. Maybe I'm doing it wrong.

Hoot! Night Owl!
by **Marco Angeles**
aka **ivejustquitsmoking**, Philippines

Score: 3.56/5 by 706 people

08

Because nobody likes to clean up vomit.

Save the World
by **Print Liberation**, USA

Select

09

I was watching a show about dinosaurs on the History Channel a couple days ago. Dinosaurs are completely crazy.

Two Dinosaurs Caught in a Chinese Finger Trap
by **Justin White** aka **jublin**, USA

Score: 3.18/5 by 870 people

13

Seven Swans was inspired by the Sufjan Stevens album and title track.

Seven Swans
by **Priscilla Wilson**
aka **valorandvellum**, USA

Score: 3.40/5 by 1,180 people

14

It is a modest shirt. A shirt about what could have been. A shirt about Abe.

Abe
by **Joe Carr** aka **ISABOA**, USA

Score: 3.06/5 by 911 people

15

This image is so subtle. OXEN.'s digital painter—DJ mash-up—for the masses, by the masses.

Three Keyboard Cat Moon
by **Emilee Seymour** and **Shawn Harris**
aka **OXEN.**, USA/Australia

Score: 4.48/5 by 3,791 people

04

I really liked the way the feathers came out on my Mayan/Aztec dude for my Select design *Leader*, and thought it would be cool to have a shirt of all feathers. At first I was just going to be lazy and copy and paste the vectors from the Select file. But I decided I wanted more of a hand-drawn feel.

Feathered Fringe

by **Joe Van Wetering** aka **speedyjvw**, USA

Score: 3.04/5 by 632 people

I have always loved the look of the classic 1980s van, like the one used on *The A-Team*. So I thought it would be fun to see what other famous movie and TV vehicles would be like if they were cast as a van.

It Would Have Been Cooler as a Van

by **Brandon Ortwein** aka **bortwein**, USA

Score: 3.24/5 by 779 people

A friend had really long hair. Someone mentioned she could wear it as a t-shirt and that image stuck in my mind. I tried a few ideas, but I liked the intricate line work and large format.

Her Hair

by **Federico Rodriguez Morice** aka **FFico**, Costa Rica

Score: 2.66/5 by 1,994 people

I was wondering how to combine two famous optical illusions—the Penrose triangle and the devil's tuning fork—in one graphic. Suddenly a miracle happened and they joined together perfectly!

Untitled: Impossible

by **Tang Yau Hoong** aka **TangYauHoong**, Malaysia

Score: 2.75/5 by 718 people

The stars in the sky always disappear for a while. I'm always thinking maybe someone stole them and brought them back to light up their home.

Sky Thief

by **Chow Hon Lam** aka **Flying Mouse 365**, Malaysia

Score: 3.15/5 by 658 people

They are back, new times, new rules.

HEARTLESS

by **Juan Carlos Bueno** aka **ounom**, Spain

Score: 3.92/5 by 735 people

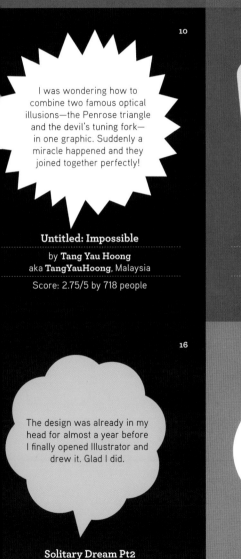

The design was already in my head for almost a year before I finally opened Illustrator and drew it. Glad I did.

Solitary Dream Pt2

by **Budi Satria Kwan** aka **radiomode**, Singapore

Score: 3.46/5 by 917 people

A bizarre mix of contemporary cyclops and ridiculously normal vehicles was the main idea.

3 Eyes, 3 Vehicles

by **Daniel Abensour** aka **Aphte**, France

Score: 2.76/5 by 911 people

I like that all skulls are smiling. We are all smiling inside, even if we are frowning on the outside.

Frowns Are Flesh

by **Geoff McFetridge**, USA

Select

INSANE AMAZINGNESS

Even though Threadless is one of the first and best examples of a "crowdsourcing" business model (as we learned in 2005), we try not to think of ourselves that way. The term feels cold to us, like outsourcing work to a faceless crowd of people. We are much more about real community, friendships, and working on a fun, cool project together with your friends. It's not work: there are no specifications. It's about creating art first, and whether or not it's appropriate to be a product comes second. Threadless started as a hobby among a group of friends with a common interest, and we plan to keep it that way.

So in 2009 we hit the trenches. We want Threadless to be someone you want to be friends with, and we want it to be as easy as possible for our friends to interact with us on a one-on-one level. So we started getting really into Twitter and Facebook. On Twitter we are constantly posting what's going on at Threadless, running contests, and spreading the love. On our Facebook page it's great that we can post updates and get instant feedback from our fans. We're always screwing around with our page, making new

tabs for various things we have going on. Both are super-nice, loose ways to keep conversations going with our community. That is priceless to us. We also keep active on other sites, such as Flickr and MySpace. Chances are, if you're on a site where you interact with your friends, we're there too.

We began introducing a series of artist programs. We started a scholarship scheme, where artists whose designs are chosen for printing can accept a $3,000 scholarship instead of the $2,000 cash prize. Threadless 101 was set up as a way for teachers to bring Threadless into the classroom. And best of all, our annual Bestee award became monthly. We teamed up with Adobe to give artists a free copy of Creative Suite and another $2,000 cash if their design was chosen as the best t-shirt of the month based on popular vote. Of course, Bestee winners still received their sparkling gold Bestee medal of honor.

We also scored a couple of design challenges with museums: the New Museum in NYC and Tate Modern in London. This was huge for artists—to submit their work and have the chance of it being displayed in a museum. ▶

01

ON TWITTER WE ARE CONSTANTLY POSTING WHAT'S GOING ON, RUNNING CONTESTS, AND SPREADING THE LOVE

02

01 Joe Van Wetering proudly poses in front of his gallery opening at the Threadless store.

02 A custom deck of cards on display at the Black Rock Collective show, also held at the store. Each card was designed by a different artist.

01

The annual meet-up this year was a mega success. Our third Family Reunion was over a full weekend and included presentations from three Threadless artists, screen-printing demos from our printers, a world-record attempt by myself for most tees worn at the same time, a live t-shirt design competition by two incredible teams of artists, free Family Reunion t-shirts for all, and a hilarious beer and karaoke after-party. The Renegade Craft Fair's stop in Chicago always coincides with our meet-up, so we took a trip down there as well.

In 2009 we also made a few changes to our online store. We completely redesigned our catalog page, introducing new ways to easily browse, like color, categories, size, and price. You can even browse by awesomeness. We started designating certain Threadless designs as "Classics," always keeping them in stock. And we introduced a new type of sale, the 24-hour $9 sale. Everyone LOVED the $9 sales. The $9 sale on Black

Friday (the Friday following Thanksgiving, and start of the Christmas shopping season) was by far our biggest sales day since the beginning of Threadless.

We started to seriously explore putting Threadless designs on other products. We had done this on a smaller scale earlier on, but this year we put some real effort into making it happen. By the end of the year, we had launched a great partnership with Griffin, selling iPhone cases. They were in all the Apple stores and were an enormous hit. This is great exposure for the artists, not to mention another bump in their pocketbooks for each new product their design gets printed on. We're hoping to do more of this—working with partners to create products with Threadless art that provide an amazing canvas for it. After all, Threadless began as a t-shirt company simply because t-shirts are an easy canvas for the art.

Two folks who had been with Threadless for quite some time moved on in 2009, and I must give them a

massive thanks in this book. Jeffrey had been with us for seven years, and helped Threadless grow into what it has become today in more ways than I can count. Luckily, he still acts as an advisor to Threadless. Harper started as a developer and assumed the role of chief technology officer in 2007 after Jacob left. He has a magical connection with computers that is difficult to understand. He is an entrepreneur at heart, and I've always felt a combination of surprise and thankfulness that he stuck with Threadless as long as he did. This is a dude to watch closely if you're interested in insane amazingness.

And I must give a huge shout out to the most amazing little dude, Dash, who was born at the end of 2009. You're a trooper, little man.

OUR THIRD FAMILY REUNION INCLUDED MY WORLD-RECORD ATTEMPT FOR MOST TEES WORN

01 At our 2009 meet-up, I attempted to break the record for most shirts worn (237). I managed 166!

02 Multiple cut-outs of Craig, which we used for a sweet video.

03 We bought this Airstream on eBay, completely gutted it, and built an office inside. Today it's used as a conference room.

GAMING TEES

We've always had a bit of a nerdy/geeky audience, so I'm surprised gaming tees didn't catch on sooner. These tees are all hilarious new twists on classic video games and characters.

Jake Nickell

Shoot the Baddies

by **Olly Moss** aka **Woss**, UK

Score: 3.60/5 by 1,022 people

The Gaming Revolution

by **Sean Mort** aka **stothemofob**, UK

Score: 2.99/5 by 780 people

Alien Autopsy

by **Chris Rowson**, UK

Score: 3.63/5 by 837 people

They're Real

by **Jean Salamin** aka **okbelzoreil**, Switzerland

Score: 2.90/5 by 679 people

A Simple Plan

by **Neil Gregory** aka **NGee**, UK

Score: 2.95/5 by 1,147 people

Zombie Nomz (opposite)

by **Ken Marshall** aka **kennybanzai**, USA

Score: 2.95/5 by 567 people

The Horde (above)

by **Aled Lewis** aka **fatheed**, UK

Score: 3.74/5 by 828 people

WHO KNOWS BEST?

Karen Wong

FOR CENTURIES, WHAT IS DEEMED ART HAS BEEN FRAMED BY CHURCHES, ROYAL AND WEALTHY FAMILIES, AND MORE RECENTLY, THOSE WHO HOLD MULTIPLE ACADEMIC DEGREES.

The "curatorial voice" continues to reign supreme—an appointed arbiter of taste wields the aesthetic power to decide what is good and bad. In its primitive distillation, the "voice" in the gallery system is the owner who gamely chooses art based on its commercial viability, while a scrupulous museum curator selects work to create a legacy. These worlds are inextricably linked and remain clubs of exclusivity.

As our communication tools become more sophisticated and affordable, there is a simmering cultural shift of who gets to determine what is good. It's a buzz that permeates the airwaves—catchphrases include "the people's choice," "viewer voting," and "audience award." In the last decade, the "chorus of the community" decides who is the best pop singer of the year, or which film is poised for wider distribution. A jury of distinguished colleagues from the field remains intact—choosing the participating contestants—and then an emotionally invested public votes for a winner.

Much has been made regarding the innovative Threadless business model: crowdsourcing a retail product. Equally noteworthy, and less discussed, has been its process of circumventing normal avenues of arbitrating aesthetics and allowing emerging artists, illustrators, and designers a platform to test their talent out of reach from art school/art industry politics. This democratic approach to decide what is good (a printed tee) has been handsomely rewarded with a vast online community, millions of dollars in profit, and thousands of fulfilled artists who have seen their work produced with prize money to boot.

Rick Devos, a Michigan-based entrepreneur, took a page from the Threadless playbook when he created the ArtPrize in 2009. Touted as the richest purse for a visual arts award ($250,000 for the winner), the ArtPrize has an open call for submissions, and voting takes place in two phases when the public views the work in situ at numerous venues across Grand Rapids, Devos's hometown. Voter registration stations are set up across the city, and the explicit manifesto is to give the "public an empowering voice in responding to the art."[01] Devos claims not to be anti-jury or anti-curator; rather the competition is a new social experiment.[02]

Threadless (the name is "both a play on thread—either a clothing item or a discussion topic on an online forum"[03]) was founded on a similar notion. Expanding the conversation is a consistent theme for both these Midwestern initiatives. And perhaps more than anything else, these Internet leaders have tapped into a disenfranchised public that want their opinions to matter . . . and to be counted.

footnotes
01 artprize.org/people
02 artprize.org/mission
03 inc.com/magazine/20080601/the-customer-is-the-company.html

Karen Wong founded Hobbamock Design, a graphic design firm committed to non-profits and social causes, in the early 1990s. In 2000 she became managing director of Adjaye/Associates, a young architectural studio, based in London. In 2006 she became the first director of external affairs for the New Museum of Contemporary Art in NYC. She has art directed numerous architecture and art books, and designed dozens of t-shirts. Karen has yet to enter a design on Threadless.

The inspiration for this was Red Riding
Hood's revenge, an image I once saw
of a little Red in her hooding a knife
with the wolf's shadow on a wall
literally that I can't bang in my version
protects the little Red wolf, with a very
bloody background.

The Red
by Dina Prasetyawan aka kooky.love, Indonesia
Score 2.99/5 by 1,009 people

Location: Madison, WI, USA

Member since June 2003

If I could be friends with any cartoon character of course it would be Sailor Moon, from the Japanese anime series about a team of magical girls. Actually, maybe Sailor Mercury, because she was the quiet, nerdy sailor scout of the group, and I always related more to her. I would want to borrow her Virtual Boy–esque headset. Sailor Saturn was also cool, because she was so goth.

Like most artists, I've drawn since I was young. A lot from life, and way too much Sailor Moon. I grew up in suburban Georgia, among kudzu vines and dogwood trees. In high school I began discovering textbook abstract and modern artists, and my perception of art completely changed. I discovered graphic design, and was a layout designer for my school paper, too.

I love making both art and music, and have phases of creating both. In a way, creating music is more satisfying, because there's more potential to appropriate styles and develop new sounds to create something that hasn't been heard before. Whereas with art it's difficult to come up with something substantially unique. Not saying you can't do that with art, but I've personally felt more confident in my music, in that sense.

I'm terrible at taking care of my art. I draw directly on the computer because it's the best way to ensure it won't just get crumpled up and thrown into the trash. I usually draw everything in Photoshop. Similarly, when working on music, I usually record all my ideas right away in Pro Tools. ▸

JULIA HEGLUND *aka* SONMI

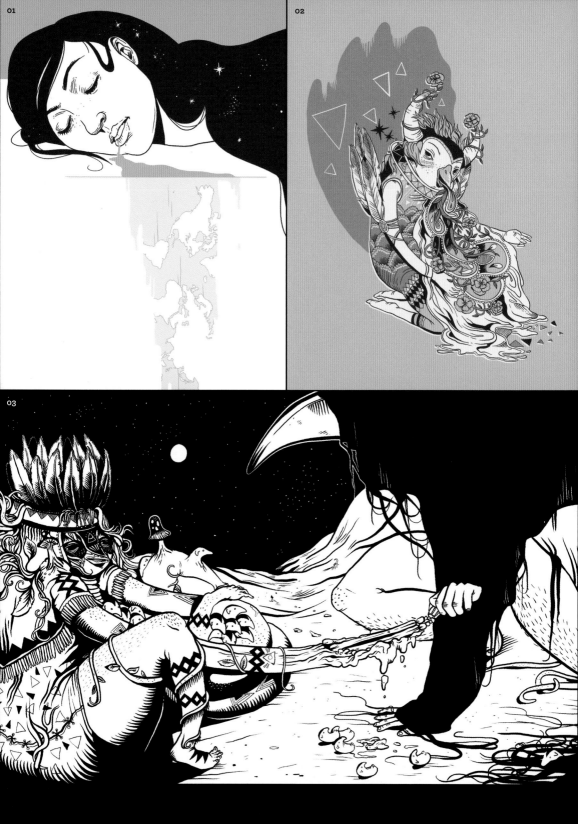

01

02

03

04

01 **The Great Slumber**
(personal work)
02 **Bird King**
(Kingstrike)
03 **Doomsday**
(*Faesthetic* magazine)
04 **Yesterday's Breakfast**
(exclusive for this book)

You can see one of Julia's
Threadless designs on
page 73 (04).

When I found Threadless it became like an addiction. It's a rare community, in that its members are super-friendly, passionate about art, and just really cool and diverse. As Priscilla, aka valorandvellum, once said: "Threadless people are awesome because they plan super-cool trips and actually make it happen!" Because of Threadless, I've traveled to San Diego, San Francisco, Las Vegas, New York, and Toronto. I can't wait for our next trip. Sign me up for the future!

My art friends are some of my favorite artists. Otherwise, I'd love to own a print of Will Bryant's slogan, "I Love Nice People Who Make Cool Things," because I can't think of a phrase that has more distinctly resonated with me. *Folk Rock and Roll*, *Untitled* and *Hadrian* are my favorite designs from other Threadless artists.

During college I began to think about artistic styles, with influences from artists I discovered online. Anyone from Graphic Havoc to Seripop. Eventually, I became more confident in a style I was developing, and decided to submit a design to Threadless.

Lots of people think "sonmi" is an alias—it's actually my middle name.

I can never pass up a good squeaky cheese curd. My home is now in America's Dairyland of Wisconsin. I've always been partial to Bucky Badger brand port wine cheese spread too. I feel more obliged to like that one—Bucky is the mascot of my alma mater, the University of Wisconsin-Madison. Oh man! I haven't had that stuff in forever. I need to go grocery shopping. . . .

I HATE YOU, BIKE THIEF

The design was based on some flyers I put up when my bike was stolen. I later found out it had actually been impounded for being chained to a fence with a "No Bikes" sign on it. Oops! By the time my bike was recovered, the wheels were already in motion (terrible pun intended) and *Missing!!!* was on its way to becoming a shirt. The design touched a nerve with enough people that Threadless started ihateyoubikethief.com, where people like me shared the pain, grief, and all-encompassing sense of loss that comes with having a bike stolen. (Or, in my case, misplaced and presumed stolen.) **Julian Glander**

Missing!!!
by **Julian Glander** aka **secretly robots**, USA
Score: 3.10/5 by 610 people

MISSING!!!

(DRAWN FROM MEMORY.
MAY NOT BE TO SCALE.)

20 INCHES

MY BIKE WAS STOLEN FROM MY
FRONT LAWN LAST WEEK. IT IS A
ONE-SPEED BIKE WITH A SKULL FLAG
AND A LIGHTNING BOLT ON IT. THE
LIGHTNING BOLT AND FLAG MAY HAVE
BEEN REMOVED. THIS BIKE WAS
BRAND NEW FROM THE STORE.

NO REWARD

I DON'T EVEN WANT THIS BIKE BACK.
I JUST MADE THESE FLYERS TO TELL
YOU THAT I HATE YOU, BIKE THIEF.
I HOPE YOU RIDE MY BIKE WITHOUT
A HELMET AND GET HIT BY A MONSTER
TRUCK. I HOPE MY BIKE TAKES YOU
STRAIGHT TO HELL.

THE MISERY MACHINE

We've Got Some Work to Do Now (opposite)
by **Travis Pitts** aka **travis76**, USA
Score: 3.92/5 by 1,134 people

Springfield Still Life (above)
by **Alvaro Arteaga Sabaini** aka **alvarejo**, Chile
Score: 3.89/5 by 873 people

2009 PEOPLE'S CHOICE

I love this shirt with all of my heart and soul. I love it so hard, I'm going to cut off both arms and sell them to magical arm merchants who somehow have the power to print *It's Toile About You* on every shirt in existence. This is the only shirt that exists for me now. I even kissed it a few minutes ago. The power of this shirt is intoxicating.

Julie Bergman aka **feebsicle**

It's Toile About You

by **Emmy Cicierega** aka **EmmyCic**, USA

Score: 3.84/5 by 1,388 people

01

I thought it would be cool to re-create a Donkey Kong screen using acrylics. The graphics are so timeless and iconic that the game still maintains its identity even when slapped down quickly in paint.

Arcade Expressionism

by **Brock Davis** aka **Laser Bread**, USA

Score: 2.74/5 by 677 people

02

There's not much to say—I like bears.

Bear

by **Sebastian Gomez de la Torre** aka **Salamanderlich**, USA

Score: 3.02/5 by 837 people

03

I love simplicity. This idea combines my two favorite things: typography and food. From the colors to the typeface, this is one of my juiciest designs. Medium-rare, please.

Burgervetica

by **David Schwen** aka **dschwen**, USA

Score: 3.02/5 by 703 people

07

I hate war just as much as I love the challenge of making trite imagery seem fresh again.

Peace

by **Andy Gonsalves** aka **andyg**, USA

Score: 3.01/5 by 717 people

08

It's crazy to have a fish with an umbrella for protection because everybody knows that fish live in water. I love strange and poetic situations. I hope everybody sees that in this picture.

Glou-glou

by **Julien Canavezes** aka **djudju**, France

Score: 3.02/5 by 723 people

09

I love highly detailed illustrations, and I also like the sea. So my illustration is full of details—sailors, waves, sea animals, and all the other good stuff. It's also inspired by Japanese woodcuts of waves. And that's it—my version of a crazy sea life!

Lose Your Mind!

by **Martin Krusche** aka **MartinK.**, German

Score: 3.20/5 by 575 people

13

2009 was Charles Darwin's 200th birthday, and the 150th anniversary of *The Origin of Species*. We thought about the Pokémon creatures, how they "evolve," and imagined an alternative reality where Darwin had formulated his theory based on collecting and studying the fighting monsters.

Endless Forms Most Battleful

by **Santiago Sanchez** and **Sam McNally** aka **Santo76** and **Bio-bot 9000**, Argentina/USA

Score: 3.83/5 by 871 people

14

I love tee designs that emphasize beauty, simplicity, and wearability, and I think there should be more in the world. Inspired by the paintings of Claude Monet and the sketchbooks of Sara Midda.

Notes from Monet

by **Alice X. Zhang** aka **silverqe**, USA

Score: 2.88/5 by 663 people

15

This design comes from elementary school daydreaming, thinking about what would have happened to Columbus if his epic guess about the world was wrong. Everyone warned him he'd fall off the edge of the horizon. What would happen if they were right?

Columbus Was Wrong

by **Nicholas Tassone** aka **band-it**, USA

Score: 3.33/5 by 674 people

This design came about from a desire to draw a retro cosmonaut in a new way, and to add some fun. Initially I thought the air tube looked like a garden hose, and the rest just popped into my head, as random ideas usually do for me. And this is as random as it gets!

Shared Space
by **Blair Sayer** aka **Mr Rocks**, New Zealand

Score: 3.24/5 by 671 people

I try my best to draw funny and surrealist designs, and it's a real pleasure to make people smile. Clichés always inspire me. I have to admit that I love silliness, but you already know that.

Donuts Love Policemen
by **Florent Bocognani** aka **choubaka360**, France

Score: 3.15/5 by 719 people

My inner geek just loves the concept of recursion. Hence the small story of a fisherman in a bottle, finding himself over and over again. I wonder what he thinks at this very moment.

Fisherman's Find
by **Esther Aarts** aka **gumbolimbo**, Netherlands

Score: 3.38/5 by 732 people

Nature and music are big inspirations. Listening to music just brings visions running through my head. The owl with the fiddle was actually a character from an earlier design of mine. I wanted to do more with it and this is what emerged.

Music of the Night
by **Nichole Lillian Humphrey** aka **ratkiss**, USA

Score: 3.16/5 by 678 people

Drawing the big clumsy rhino driving the little car was awesome. I like having ideas for shirt designs, but it's getting hands-on with these little details that make it fun and worth the effort.

Overcompensating
by **Henrique Lima** aka **Tenso Graphics**, Brazil

Score: 3.08/5 by 695 people

I was thinking about weathered and decayed surfaces and wanted to show how beauty decays over time. Also, zombies are cool.

Zombie at Tiffany's
by **Marion Cromb** aka **drwhofreak**, UK

Score: 2.98/5 by 785 people

All the media buzz about Conan O'Brien inspired me to do this design and represent Conan as the new hero.

Late Night Barbarian
by **Enkel Dika** aka **buko**, Macedonia

Score: 3.61/5 by 941 people

Space is a colorless place. But with the help of hippie astronauts everything will change. This design was created thanks to my friends Virginia and Nickolas, who gave me a watercolor set as a present.

Space Needs Color
by **Alvaro Arteaga Sabaini** aka **alvarejo**, Chile

Score: 3.69/5 by 869 people

18

Pet Sounds was inspired by the strange variety of beautiful and mysterious noises animals use to express themselves. I wondered what a new kind of creature would say if it could communicate in a way we humans could understand. As it turns out—nothing profound.

Pet Sounds
by **Ben Foot** aka **B 7**, UK

Score: 3.22/5 by 690 people

AN AWESOME DECADE

Here we are! Year ten. The year that we decided to make a book about all of this madness. And because this is a book, which takes time to print and ship and all of that, I'm having to write this way back in May. It feels strange to be looking ahead at all that we have planned, wanting it all to happen, having such big ideas of what we want to do, but not knowing exactly what will happen. I'm sure there will be some big, unexpected surprises and additions to what we've got in mind by the time this book hits the shelves. The only way to really know what all went down in 2010 is to go check out the site—so . . . go check out the site!

A lot of new people have joined our staff at Threadless in the past couple of years and we felt we needed to make sure it was clear to everyone what we are trying to do. So, early in 2010, we announced our first-ever mission statement: "Inspire awesomeness." The idea being that we should always be doing things that make our community look and say: "Wow, Threadless is awesome." This idea pretty much frames everything we've got in store for this year and beyond.

For the summer we've planned a tour across the USA. With a van and an Airstream trailer, we'll make stops at music festivals, parades, and conventions like Comic-Con, and drop by in small towns to say hi to the many friends of Threadless.

Meanwhile, back at the office, our team went to work on the website. We started to overhaul the "Participate" section, completely reimagining features as if they were built today, rather than ten years ago. On the tech side, we built an API (Application Programming Interface) so that we could easily bring Threadless to other devices, social websites, and partners. We also needed to do a lot of heavy-lifting with our database set-up, but I won't bore you with all that. To top it off, we launched a bunch of international sites in different languages. Finally! Half our orders go outside of the US and we haven't really done anything special for those customers until now.

At the time of writing, we're planning to move our Chicago offices to an old FedEx distribution center in the West Loop. Basically, it's a huge warehouse with office space attached. This should really help out as we've been stretched thin on space spread across two facilities, and doing multiple daily runs back and forth between warehouses to stock up. ▸

EARLY IN 2010,
WE ANNOUNCED OUR
FIRST-EVER MISSION
STATEMENT

01 Another huge mural painted by Joe Suta. This one was completed for our new Boulder office in one night between the wee hours of 10 pm and 6 am.

02 Joe Van Wetering bangs out some logo ideas for our tenth anniversary.

01

Another thing we started doing this year that has been super-fun for us staffers is "DIY Day." We do these throughout the year: the whole company comes together and forms into small groups to work together on projects. Anyone can come up with a project. It could be a new feature on the site, a charity project, or even a completely new way of doing things like picking designs for print. These have been ridiculously fun and productive—who knows, maybe we'll just run the whole company like this in the future!

We bring the awesomeness into everything we do, no matter how small. A sample sale website called Gilt Groupe wanted to do something with us so we produced an entirely new line of high-end tees, launching them there. We started talking to an Eisner Award–winning comic book artist, Jill Thompson, and ended up creating an entire comic printed on the front and back of four t-shirts designed by four different amazing comic book artists. Also, we started working

with our community in a more official way, promoting certain members who are working on cool projects within the community to "Ambassador" level. One member is creating a book from a thread in our forum that showcases printed Threadless designs back when they were just sketches.

So far this year, one of the most exciting things is our progress in creating more opportunities for artists. Even though we have had nearly 100,000 artists submit designs to Threadless, only a small percentage of them have ever been printed. I've always wanted to do more for a greater number of the artists. This year we began to make some of that come true. Whether it's more designs printed through Threadless, or a t-shirt marketplace, commercial opportunities through partnerships, or just legitimate promotion for artists, there are a million ways we can help, and I'm stoked to be spending serious time making this happen.

THREADLESS IS A LIVING, BREATHING COMMUNITY OF PEOPLE THAT CAN'T BE TOLD WHAT TO DO

What's in store for the next ten years? Who knows? It would really be ridiculous for us to try to guess or to craft it one way or the other. Threadless is a living, breathing community of people that can't be told what to do. We listen. And we adapt and grow, embracing the change that our community wants to see. One thing's for certain—this will continue to happen over the next ten years.

That about wraps things up! I'd like to give a huge shout out to the artists, staffers (many of whom are modeling tees in the photography throughout this book), bloggers, scorers, and everyone else who has helped make Threadless what it is. Thanks for reading, and if you aren't hanging out on Threadless already, come join the fun!

Ode to Doing Nothing (opposite)

by **Joe Skec** aka **esskayeesee**, Japan

Score: 1.91/5 by 676 people

The Beach (above)

by **Lim Heng Swee** aka **ilovedoodle**, Malaysia

Score: 2.90/5 by 642 people

TREND TEES

When we ran a $10,000 competition looking for the new trend, we ended up printing ten unique creations that would shape the designs in the year to come. Here are five of our favorites! **Jake Nickell**

Diver No. 12

by **Eric Zelinski** aka **xiv**, USA

Score: 2.93/5 by 896 people

Shapeshifting Turtle

by **Skylar Hogan** aka **the Sleeping Sky**, USA

Score: 2.63/5 by 758 people

Kite Parkour

by **David Fleck** aka **Fleck**, UK

Score: 3.08/5 by 650 people

Pros & Cons

by **Aled Lewis** aka **fatheed**, UK

Score: 2.88/5 by 753 people

Firelight Cottage

by **Nathan Stillie** aka **ndstillie**, USA

Score: 3.54/5 by 912 people

RELIEF TEES

After Hurricane Katrina hit in 2005, I felt helpless living in Chicago, having recently moved from Louisiana. So I immediately talked with Jake and Jacob about designing a shirt to raise funds for the relief efforts. They were absolutely for it. I designed the shirt quickly and we got it up on the site soon after. When I heard about the earthquake in Haiti, I felt we should do another relief tee. So we contacted two printed designers from the neighboring nation of the Dominican Republic. The end product is a meaningful design based on the Haitian proverb *Men anpil chay pa lou*, which translates as "Many hands make the load lighter." We donated our total proceeds, which amounted to over $100,000. Our humble t-shirt community can raise a nice chunk of change for a worthy cause. **Ross Zietz**

Regrowth: Katrina (above)

by **Ross Zietz** aka **arzie13**, USA

Many Hands Make the Load Lighter (opposite)

by **Thomas De Santis** and **Ivan Tarrazo Sanchez** aka **Montro** and **Ivantobealone**, Dominican Republic

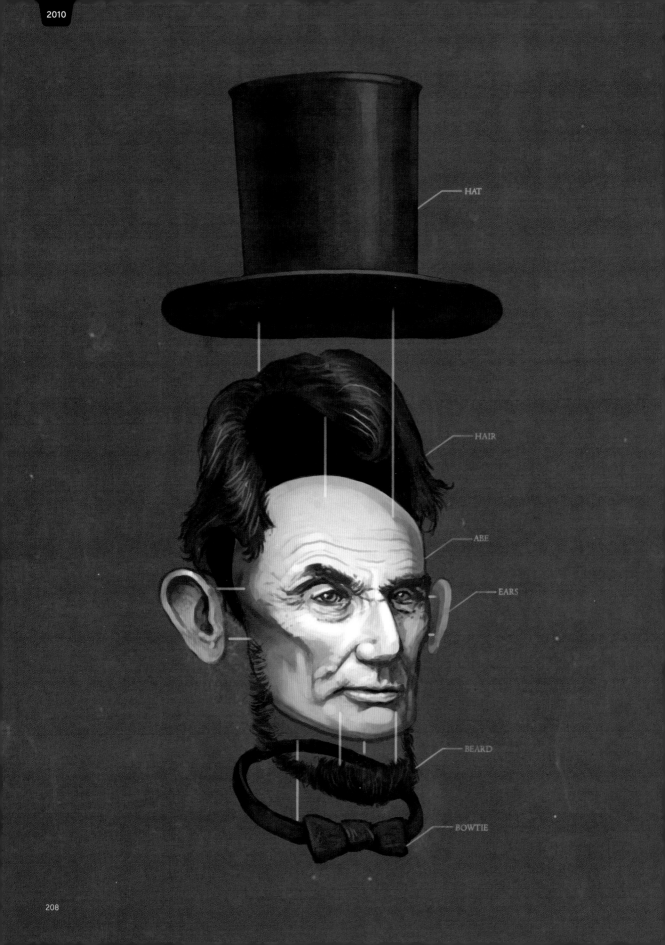

HAT

HAIR

ABE

EARS

BEARD

BOWTIE

Emancipation Schematication (opposite)

by **Mike Mitchell** aka **SirMitchell**, USA

Score: 3.23/5 by 851 people

God Save the Villain! (above)

by **Enkel Dika** aka **buko**, Macedonia

Score: 3.53/5 by 911 people

BE AMAZING BE REVOLUTIONARY!

Blake Mycoskie

BE THE ABSOLUTE WORST
WIDGET I'VE EVER SEEN!
JUST DON'T BE ORDINARY.

Threadless is a remarkable company. My favorite marketer, Seth Godin (see pages 28–29), uses the word "remarkable" not as a synonym for "exceptional" or "amazing" but in the context of something that is worthy of being remarked on. Seth calls these types of companies and ideas "purple cows." He writes: "Cows, once you've seen them for a while, are boring. They may be perfect cows, attractive cows, cows with great personalities, cows lit by beautiful light, but they're still boring. A Purple Cow, though. Now that would be interesting (for a while)."

The common bond between TOMS Shoes and Threadless is that we both strive to create meaning for our supporters beyond being a customer—whether it's by showing them how their purchases can make a difference for children in need, or by showing them how their ideas can have an impact on the design community.

The Threadless model is simple, yet revolutionary: Artists submit designs that, by the nature of the selection process, must be clever/different/innovative to stand out from the pack; the community sparks conversations about the ideas that they like best; and to complete the cycle, Threadless listens to these conversations, and prints the shirts with the most fanfare and buzz. Wash, rinse, and repeat. Because of this unique model, Threadless transforms its customers into both fans and evangelists.

A "customer" is a nameless and faceless person with a credit card, someone who buys your product because it's the cheapest, or perhaps the most convenient option. As circumstances change, customers take their purchasing dollars elsewhere, and more often than not, leave no trace behind—not even an angry rant. No one blogs or tweets about things that are average.

When Threadless releases new shirts every week, there is never any doubt whether their products will be remarkable because the tribe has, in fact, already spoken. Every shirt carries with it its own unique story: Somewhere in the world, an artist has been turned into a t-shirt entrepreneur. A legion of fans can blog, Facebook and tweet that their vote made this shirt possible; and even the most casual fan can feel like they've discovered something new and fresh.

When TOMS first began in 2006, we were (pardon the pun) working on a shoestring budget. We could never afford to advertise in magazines, pay department stores to display our product, or gift shoes to celebrities. I would like to say that I knew what I was doing, but I had absolutely no experience in either footwear or fashion. About the only thing that we did have was a story: With every pair you purchase, TOMS will give a pair of new shoes to a child in need. One for One. There are no percentages or formulas, just simple One for One giving.

This story, like the unique business model pioneered by Threadless, has turned TOMS' customers into fans and evangelists. Ask a TOMS' fan what type of shoes she's wearing and you'll almost certainly get more than a one-word answer. She may tell you about our beginnings in Argentina, a Shoe Drop she attended, or a rad design-your-own party that her friends threw on campus. The beauty of TOMS, and of companies like Threadless, is that every customer adds their own unique perspective to the collective story.

Blake Mycoskie is the founder and Chief Shoe Giver of TOMS Shoes. He founded TOMS following a trip to Argentina in 2006 when he was struck by the number of children without shoes to protect them. His One for One model has provided more than 600,000 pairs of shoes to children around the world. Blake is a recipient of the Cooper-Hewitt People's Design Award and the Secretary of State's Award for Corporate Excellence (ACE).

Streetlife (opposite)

by **Peter Goes** aka **Anything Goes**, Belgium

Score: 3.54/5 by 587 people

INKspired (above)

by **Seth Beukes** aka **sethdesign**, South Africa

Score: 2.97/5 by 584 people

Spoiled Milk (opposite)

by **Joshua Kemble** and **Mike Getsiv**
aka **polynothing** and **GetsiVizioN**, USA

Score: 3.12/5 by 614 people

BOOM BOX (above)

by **Alex Solis**
aka **alexmdc**, USA

Score: 3.61/5 by 799 people

Location: Struga, Macedonia

Member since February 2008

I've been drawing for as long as I can remember. As a kid I drew a lot of cartoon characters, and I wanted to be an animator. But then my dream was to become an astronaut who has superpowers, which would be really cool. I'm not sure why I haven't chased my dream yet.

I discovered Threadless while browsing some design blogs. Initially I began submitting to smaller sites because I felt I wasn't ready for Threadless. Then I saw the Loves Moby competition on Threadless—I was so excited I had to submit something. Even though I got a low score, it quickly became my new addiction.

Finally, after five submissions, I won the Loves Drawing competition. I can't describe how excited I was—I was screaming and bouncing all over the place. Getting printed is so important to me. The fact that somebody loves my designs motivates me to work even harder.

My design process is pretty much the same every time—sketch . . . scan . . . Photoshop. It takes a lot of time to finish my designs because I'm such a perfectionist and I'm never completely satisfied with the result. Every time one of my designs is chosen for printing I always have to make one more final change!

I really enjoy the challenge and satisfaction of collaborating with other talented and amazing people in the Threadless community. I've had some great experiences with FRICKINAWESOME, silverqe, and mark722. ▸

ENKEL DIKA *aka* BUKO

01

I'm planning to do a collab with the extremely talented alexmdc. Something like *Clash of the Titans* would work perfectly, but he doesn't know about it yet.

I've never had a particular style. The challenge of working in different styles means I'm always reinventing and improving my work. The community's positive reaction has helped me to evolve as a designer. Most of my designs are complex and with lots of details, although I wish I was better at simpler designs. After all, simplicity is the ultimate sophistication.

I've never been influenced by any one particular artist or designer, but I've always enjoyed the work of Wassily Kandinsky, Salvador Dalí, M. C. Escher, Yuta Onoda, Paul Rand, Jason Munn, Chema Madoz, Andy Gilmore, and many others.

Creativity has always been a part of my life and I find inspiration in everything around me, including good music, nature, and movies. I'm currently addicted to pop culture references in my work. I also have a lot of animal-themed designs. I love all animals except chickens, which seem kind of stupid.

A friend came up with "Buko," my aka. Basically, it's a play on the word for bread in Albanian (one of his nicknames for me was Ekmek, which means bread in Turkish).

Some of my favorite Threadless designs are Select tees including *Leader*, *Dead Pirate*, and *Thanks for Everything*. If I had to choose one design that best represents me it would probably be *Swinging Away*. It might not be my best design, but it's really special to me and it's dedicated to my sister, the most precious person in my life.

Warrior's Pet (opposite)

by **Kim Mak**, Singapore

Score: 2.29/5 by 666 people

Holidays (above)

by **Maxime Francout** aka **Max F**, Canada

Score: 2.14/5 by 641 people

INDEX OF DESIGNERS

Numbers in parentheses refer to images on multi-tee pages

Designs for year openers:

2000–2004 **Ctrl + Z** by **Ben Devens** aka **//ben.**
2005 **The Morning After** by **Paul Southworth** aka **southworth**
2006 **The Communist Party** by **Tom Burns** aka **tomburns**
2007 **Living in Harmony** by **Josh Perkins** aka **theperk**
2008 **Mister Mittens' Big Adventure** by **Joe Van Wetering** aka **speedyjvw**
2009 **Party Animal** by **John Hegquist** aka **quister**
2010 **Real Peanuts** by **Phil Jones** aka **murraymullet**

Picture credits All photographs by Threadless unless otherwise specified.

36–37 Ross Zietz by Anna Bryant in his home in Chicago, IL; 58–59 Glenn Jones by Glenn Jones and a self-timer in his garden in Auckland, New Zealand; 90–91 Olly Moss by Paul Octavious at Ross Zietz's apartment in Chicago, IL; 120–121 Chow Hon Lam by Jimmy Tan, Studio Numb9r, in his workplace in Malaysia; 148–149 Aled Lewis by Abigail Wilson at The Woolpack in London; 180–181 Julia Sonmi Heglund by Julia Sonmi Heglund in her living room in Madison, WI; 216–217 Enkel Dika by Kushtrim Shehu in Café Bar Sapphire in Struga, Macedonia.

. . . and finally, how the heck do you go about creating a cover for a

book like *Threadless*? If you lined up all the designs that have been submitted over the years they would reach to the moon and back at least eighteen times (guesstimation). We decided to make the cover a colossal collaboration and asked all of our alumni to draw a character wearing a blank tee. More than eighty artists from around the world sent in characters. We mashed up a selection of them into what you are holding in your hands now, crafting a piece that really represents the creativity, community, variety, and straight-up awesomeness that is Threadless. We couldn't include all of the amazing characters that were submitted because of space and composition limitations, but on the next page we've included the ones that didn't make it onto the cover for you to check out. I also thought the idea of having each character wear a blank t-shirt and letting the artwork be the characters themselves was quite clever—if I do say so myself! **Jake Nickell**

Here are all the artists who sent in characters: **Esther Aarts, Wenceslao Almazan, Marco Angeles, Randy Aquilizan, Jan Avendano, Frank Barbara, Andrew Bargeron, Black Rock Collective, Florent Bocognani, Vincent Bocognani, Riccardo Bucchioni, Justin Chee, William Chua, Stuart Colebrook, Jalid Deccarett, Tony Elmore, Ersin Erturk, Eric Fan, Terry Fan, Michael Valadares Ferreira, Rodrigo Ferreira, Ben Foot, Zack Maxfield Forer, Roberto Gálvez, Andy Gonsalves, Jim Gray, Jimmy Tan Wei Hau, Julia Sonmi Heglund, Samuel Lara Hernández, Skylar Hogan, Yeoh Guan Hong, Tang Yau Hoong, Aaron Jay, Danielle Kerese, Peter Kramar, Andreas Krapf, Brian Kravitz, Keith Kuniyuki, Budi Satria Kwan, Roni Lagin, Chow Hon Lam, Richard Lee, Robbie Lee, Steven Lefcourt, Ian Leino, Michelle Li, Lim Heng Swee, Jamerson Lima, Terence Mack, Hector Mansilla, Ken Marshall, Dann Matthews, Cameron McEwan, Stephanie McFeters, Edgar R. McHerly, Kneil Melicano, Amy Midkiff, A.J. Mohacsy, Jillian Nickell, Paul Odders, Brandon Ortwein, Ivan Leonardo Vera Piñeros, Dina Prasetyawan, Jennifer Raad, Gavin Rampling, Adam Rosenbaum, Danger Russ, Leon Ryan, Álvaro Arteaga Sabaini, Santiago Sanchez, Blair Sayer, Benjamin Schmitt, Alex Solis, Evan Stoler, Jared Stumpenhorst, Chris Thornley, Philip Tseng, Joe Van Wetering, Andy Walker, Brian Walline, Craig Watkins, Adam White, Justin White, Steve Wierth, Priscilla Wilson, Ross Zietz**